Deseret Book Company
Salt Lake City, Utah
1978

Printed in the United States of America

Library of Congress Cataloging in Publication Data

Petersen, Mark E.
Joshua, man of faith.
Includes index.
1. Joshua, son of Nun. 2. Bible. O.T.—Biography.
I. Title.
BS580.J7P47 222'.2'0924 78-10143
ISBN 0-87747-720-5

To
EMMA MARR
who regarded Joshua 1:9
as a sacred promise

CONTENTS

Chapter 1

FROM SLAVE TO PROPHET

One of the best loved passages in all scripture is this: "Choose you this day whom ye will serve; . . . but as for me and my house, we will serve the Lord." (Joshua 24:15.)

This challenge was spoken to ancient Israel in a time of great crisis when the people were at a crossroads: Should Israel follow the popular and seductive pagan gods of their neighbors, or should they isolate themselves and remain with the one and only true and living God who had brought them out of Egyptian bondage?

The Twelve Tribes had been rescued by the greatest series of miracles ever recorded, with the exception of the atonement and resurrection of the Savior.

They had been freed from Pharaoh's soldiers and had seen them drowned; they had crossed the Red Sea on dry land and had had food miraculously provided for them; they were given an adequate water supply in the desert, also by a miracle; and since they were not able to provide new clothing for themselves as they traveled, their wearing apparel did not wear out in many years of wandering in the wilderness.

They had seen the fiery visitation of Almighty God on Sinai and had witnessed the miracles of Moses. It was all a great reality to them, for they had lived through it all. But they also faced the seductive influence of their depraved neighbors, who were led by wicked kings instead of prophets and who had many gods for all occasions instead of the one true God.

One of the ugly things about the idolatrous neighbors was that some of their heathen gods were sex symbols whose worship included patronage of deviates. Such immorality supposedly placated the deities; instead it corrupted the patrons.

The Almighty knew what he was doing. He knew that Egypt had been both good and bad for Israel—good because it provided a refuge for four hundred years while the family of Jacob became a mighty nation, and bad because in that land the Hebrews became attracted to idolatry with all its evil perversions.

And the Lord knew, too, that he was bringing his people into a Promised Land that had been defiled by the dreadful wickedness of the pagans who resided there.

So he made every effort to fortify Israel against this evil. He had promised Abraham that he would bring Abraham's children into this land of milk and honey to fulfill their divine destiny; but a severe cleansing process throughout the land would have to precede it. And God's people would themselves have to be fortified against paganism in their own thinking and in their own faith.

It seems that all through the ages idolatry had been associated with perversions of some kind. It was so in Greece, in Egypt, in Rome, in Ephesus, and even in ancient America. Some groups even required human sacrifices.

Immorality was often introduced with rituals as a necessary part of pagan worship. What could please the devil more than to persuade people that perversion was allowed by their religion, knowing full well that this deception would drag them quickly down to hell?

Corruption of religion and a collapse of morals readily go hand in hand and form a fatal trap for the gullible and the foolish.

It is no wonder that the Lord brought his people to Mount Sinai to receive his stern but necessary lesson on idolatry and immorality. He not only gave Israel the Ten Commandments then, but as part of the law of Moses he later gave further laws against evil sex practices, including homosexuality. He provided the death penalty in many instances when his laws were violated.

He previously had struck down Sodom and Gomorrah, destroying them completely. The people of Canaan were like the Sodomites in their wickedness and would have to be destroyed from before the face of the Lord. Not only would their destruction cleanse the area, but it would also make room for the people whom God hoped to rear there in righteousness.

Hence it was that when he brought the Israelites into the Promised Land the Lord commanded them to wipe out its evil occupants, with their property and all vestiges of idolatry; to slay men, women, and children; to burn the cities. The cleansing must be complete.

So he raised up Joshua, the son of Nun, a former Israelitish slave from Egypt, to be the leader of this undertaking.

Moses had worried about the selection of a successor, since he knew that he himself was not to be allowed to lead Israel into the Promised Land.

> And Moses spake unto the Lord, saying,
> Let the Lord, the God of the spirits of all flesh, set a man over the congregation,
> Which may go out before them, and which may go in before them, and which may lead them out, and which may bring them in; that the congregation of the Lord be not as sheep which have no shepherd.
> And the Lord said unto Moses, Take thee Joshua the son of Nun, a man in whom is the spirit, and lay thine hand upon him;
> And set him before Eleazar the priest, and before all the congregation; and give him a charge in their sight.
> And thou shalt put some of thine honour upon him, that all the congregation of the children of Israel may be obedient.
> And he shall stand before Eleazar the priest, who shall ask counsel for him after the judgment of Urim before the Lord: at his word shall they go out, and at his word they shall come in, both he, and all the children of Israel with him, even all the congregation.
> And Moses did as the Lord commanded him: and he took Joshua, and set him before Eleazar the priest, and before all the congregation:
> And he laid his hands upon him, and gave him a charge, as the Lord commanded by the hand of Moses. (Numbers 27:15-23.)

As the new prophet in Israel, Joshua was given two objectives by the Lord: to settle the tribes in the Promised

Land, and to cleanse Canaan of both its wicked people and its sinful religion so that the region would be suitable for Jacob's children to live in.

In doing so, however, he must teach Israel to eschew idolatry and its accompanying perversions. That included wiping out idolatry's adherents, never marrying with the Canaanites, serving the one and only true and living God, and destroying the handmade images of Canaan together with the "high places" or pagan sanctuaries.

In persuading the Israelites to see the difference in the choices that were before them, the true God or the seductive idols, the prophet made this mighty appeal: "If it seem evil unto you to serve the Lord, choose you this day whom ye will serve; whether the gods which your fathers served that were on the other side of the flood [Jordan River], or the gods of the Amorites, in whose land ye dwell: but as for me and my house, we will serve the Lord." (Joshua 24:15.)

These words still stand as a mighty challenge to every person, and now especially to modern Israel.

Chapter 2

THE PLAGUE OF IDOLATRY

Joshua had been a slave in Egypt but now had become the successor to Moses in the liberation of the Twelve Tribes. At the highest pinnacle of his colorful career he had ascended Sinai with Moses when the Almighty renewed his Abrahamic promises and revealed himself personally as the one and only true and living God.

Joshua was a prophet extraordinaire. Few ever drew nearer to God than did this new leader of Israel. Yet he was a mighty warrior and a farsighted governor as well.

He was humble like Moses, who was called the meekest man on earth. He knew full well whence his power came, for the Lord himself had told him: "As I was with Moses, so I will be with thee: I will not fail thee, nor forsake thee." (Joshua 1:5.)

Constantly recognizing the Lord and bowing to his Almighty wisdom and direction, Joshua never took any credit to himself for his spectacular accomplishments. Hence, the Lord loved him. Like David who was to follow many years later, Joshua was near to God's own heart.

When the magnitude of his calling seemed to frighten him, the Lord encouraged him: "I will not fail thee. . . . Only be thou strong and very courageous, . . . that thou mayest prosper whithersoever thou goest." (Joshua 1:5, 7.)

And this was exactly how Joshua lived, never doubting the Lord, never fearful of the problems before him, always being assured that the Almighty would keep his promises.

Many lessons were taught in the Lord's call to Joshua, lessons of faith, courage, endurance, devotion, and keen attention to the detail of the Lord's commandments.

When Joshua's call first came, the Lord spoke to him

and said: "Moses my servant is dead; now therefore arise, go over this Jordan, thou, and all this people, unto the land which I do give to them, even to the children of Israel." (Joshua 1:2.)

Moses had not been allowed to lead the people over Jordan. The Lord had shown the land of promise to the great liberator and lawgiver from a mountaintop, but had kept from him the privilege of directing its occupancy. That task was assigned to Joshua, who now received the divine commission to proceed with the great undertaking.

The possession of the land was to be accompanied by miracles very similar to those performed by Moses as the tribes left Egypt. For example, the Red Sea parted at the command of Moses, and now the Jordan must obey a similar command from Joshua.

Strength and protection from heaven would attend the invading armies as they attacked and wiped out the wicked people hidden behind the thick walls of their cities.

But to be successful the Israelites must be loyal to their great Deliverer, Jehovah. By his fiery appearance on Mount Sinai the Lord had given them the law of Moses, including the Ten Commandments, in which idolatry and moral corruption were firmly denounced and forbidden. (3 Nephi 15.)

The people forever must renounce the paganism that now threatened them like a disease, contagious in the extreme. They had learned much about the evils of idolatry in Egypt, but had not given it up. This was made evident very sadly when Aaron, the brother of Moses their leader, helped them to make a golden calf, which they worshipped.

Having left the gods of Egypt behind them, they were now to face the set of false deities worshipped by the wicked Canaanites. The threat was extreme, as was their need for divine help.

Many among them had been converted to idolatry while in bondage, and this weakness still remained, despite the stern rebuke of the Lord.

When the Almighty said, "I am the Lord thy God," he meant exactly that. The words *thy God* were significant, *thy* referring to the invading Israelites who were to seek him and him alone, first, last, and always.

And when the Lord said, "Thou shalt have no other gods before me," he spoke more especially of the idols to which they were exposed, such as those that were worshipped both in Egypt and in Canaan and with which the Israelites were much too familiar already.

And when the Lord said: "Thou shalt not make unto thee any graven image, or any likeness of any thing that is in heaven above, or that is in the earth beneath, or that is in the water under the earth," he made himself clear beyond all misunderstanding.

"Thou shalt not bow down thyself to them, nor serve them," he declared, "for I the Lord thy God am a jealous God, visiting the iniquity of the fathers upon the children unto the third and fourth generation of them that hate me." (Exodus 20:1-5.)

He showed unmeasured mercy to those who loved him, but visited appropriate punishments upon those who flaunted their apostasy from the Lord in favor of idols.

Why did idolatry have such strong appeal?

The idolatry of those days, both in Canaan and throughout the Near East, was especially pernicious because it combined immorality with religion. This was true even in the days of Paul at Ephesus, when the populace cried out "Great is Diana of the Ephesians," who was herself a sex symbol, a goddess of fertility.

Idolatry in those centuries actually was a glorification of sexual deviations through religion. It combined a rejection of the true God, by turning to idols, with a repudiation of the laws of virtue laid down by the Lord. It was a double insult to him. Therefore, God had reason to be severe in his condemnation of such worship and in demanding that Israel keep the law of chastity, which under Moses provided the death penalty for its violation.

So Joshua's dual responsibility was a great one, and this he understood. Assured that his call was divine, he was certain that his work could not fail if he followed the Lord's directions.

And the Lord knew that unless the Israelites did follow his directions, they never could succeed. Cleanliness and devotion to God were the two great ingredients in his formula for achievement.

Although great efforts were made both by the Lord and by Joshua to wipe out idolatry and immorality, in the years to come these sins continually kept reappearing among various Israelites.

In the days of Rehoboam the condition became so bad that the scripture speaks of it as follows:

"And Judah did evil in the sight of the Lord, and they provoked him to jealousy with their sins which they had committed, above all that their fathers had done.

"For they also built them high places, and images, and groves, on every high hill, and under every green tree.

"And there were also sodomites in the land: and they did according to all the abominations of the nations which the Lord cast out before the children of Israel." (1 Kings 14:22-24.)

Again we see a direct relationship between sodomy, other forms of immorality, and idolatry.

Chapter 3

"ONLY BE THOU STRONG"

The Lord knew that only a tight rein on Israel would keep his people in the "strait and narrow way," for they had never recovered from their tendency to go astray.

So he warned Joshua at the very beginning of his service: "This book of the law shall not depart out of thy mouth; but thou shalt meditate therein day and night, that thou mayest observe to do according to all that is written therein: for then thou shalt make thy way prosperous, and then thou shalt have good success."

He continued with this wondrous command and promise: "Have not I commanded thee? Be strong and of a good courage; be not afraid, neither be thou dismayed: for the Lord thy God is with thee whithersoever thou goest." (Joshua 1:8-9.)

Joshua immediately commanded the people to follow the Lord's direction. They were obviously impressed and "answered Joshua, saying, All that thou commandest us we will do, and whithersoever thou sendest us, we will go.

"According as we hearkened unto Moses in all things, so will we hearken unto thee: only the Lord thy God be with thee, as he was with Moses.

"Whosoever he be that doth rebel against thy commandment, and will not hearken unto thy words in all that thou commandest him, he shall be put to death: only be strong and of a good courage." (Joshua 1:16-18.)

The scripture seems to hint that the people did not feel too secure in their new leadership. Was it with some reservation that they said they would obey Joshua only if "the Lord thy God be with thee, as he was with Moses"?

It seems that some doubt was in their minds, because

they repeated to Joshua the Lord's own reminder: "Be strong and of a good courage."

They had every right to expect strong leadership for the work the Lord now required of them. It would be difficult indeed to attack the wicked Canaanites in their well-fortified cities, some of which were surrounded by thick masonry walls.

Israel had little reason to doubt Joshua, although they knew that he was well advanced in years, and fighting was a young man's calling. By this time he was eighty or more years of age. Historians say that Joshua was forty when Moses came before Pharaoh in his miraculous confrontation. And Joshua aged another forty years as the Israelites wandered in the desert.

Joshua had proven his courage and skill, for while Moses was yet alive and before the tribes had crossed the Jordan into the Promised Land he had led them in successful battles on the east side of the river.

Joshua now lived up to every expectation. He was an ideal example of humble obedience to the Lord. He was a mighty antagonist against idolatry, and was also a revelator and a prophet for the true God.

His name is interesting. The *Encyclopaedia Judaica* says that the name means "YHWH is salvation. . . . His name was originally Hosea (Numbers 13:8, 16; Deuteronomy 32:44)." (New York: Macmillan Co., 1971, 10:266.)

The *Commentary on the Bible* by Adam Clarke explains:

"Joshua, son of Nun, of the tribe of Ephraim, was first called *Oshea* or *Hoshea* (Numbers 13:16) which signifies *saved*, a *savior*, or *salvation*, but afterward, Moses, guided no doubt by a prophetic spirit, changed his name into *Yehoshua* or *Joshua*, which signifies *he shall save* or *the salvation of Jehovah;* referring no doubt to his being God's instrument in *saving the people* from the hands of their enemies and leading them from victory to victory over the different Canaanitish nations, till he put them in possession of the promised land." (Nashville and New York: Abingdon Press, 2:3.)

Dr. William Smith's *New Dictionary of the Bible* reads: "The son of Nun, tribe of Ephraim. Born about the time that Moses fled to Midian, slave in Egypt's brick-fields, he was forty at the Exodus. . . . He was with Moses in the mount when the golden calf was made." (Garden City, New York: Doubleday, 1966, p. 194.)

This volume says that Joshua assumed command of the armies of Israel in his eighty-fifth year.

The *New Catholic Encyclopedia* says that the Bible pictures Joshua "as a man fearless in battle, not because of his own strength and courage, but because of the powerful presence of Yahweh. . . . [Joshua] stands forever in the shadow of Moses. This fact does not diminish him. It highlights his indispensable role as the man who led the people all the way into the Holy Land. Through [Joshua's] activity as well as that of Moses, Yahweh's loving fidelity was manifested as He saved His people from Egypt and the desert and brought them safely into the land He had promised to Abraham, Isaac and Jacob." (San Francisco: McGraw Hill, 1967, 7:1125-26.)

The entire career of Joshua seems to have been marked by humility, devotion, complete obedience to the Lord, and courage in battle. In addition, he was eminently fair in distributing allotments of land in Canaan among the tribes of Israel.

He was a great prophet, a wise administrator and governor, and a humble leader of the people. He stands high among all the Old Testament personalities.

Chapter 4

A FRIGHTENING LAND

Long before Joshua's call to be leader of the Israelites he showed himself to be a faithful follower of the Lord. This is seen in the events that immediately preceded the Israelites' forty-year sojourn in the wilderness.

When the Israelites were first exposed to the land of Canaan, it frightened them. They were afraid to enter. It was that lack of faith that brought upon them their forty years of wandering.

Moses sent scouts into Canaan to see what obstacles to occupying the land the Israelites faced. These men spent forty days surveying the land, and when they returned they addressed Moses and Aaron in the presence of the whole congregation, so that everyone heard their discouraging remarks. They had brought with them samples of the fruit of the land to show that it was indeed productive, but added that it was also formidable. They said:

"We came unto the land whither thou sentest us, and surely it floweth with milk and honey; and this is the fruit of it.

"Nevertheless the people be strong that dwell in the land, and the cities are walled, and very great: and moreover we saw the children of Anak there.

"The Amalekites dwell in the land of the south: and the Hittites, and the Jebusites, and the Amorites, dwell in the mountains: and the Canaanites dwell by the sea, and by the coast of Jordan." (Number 13:27-29.)

This negative report disturbed Moses, and greatly displeased one of his ablest assistants, Caleb, who "stilled the people before Moses, and said, Let us go up at once, and possess it; for we are well able to overcome it."

Some of the men who went up as scouts immediately disagreed, saying, "We be not able to go up against the people; for they are stronger than we.

"And they brought up an evil report of the land which they had searched unto the children of Israel, saying, The land, through which we have gone to search it, is a land that eateth up the inhabitants thereof; and all the people that we saw in it are men of a great stature.

"And there we saw the giants, the sons of Anak, which come of the giants: and we were in our own sight as grasshoppers, and so we were in their sight." (Numbers 13:30-33.)

So discouraging was their report that "all the congregation lifted up their voice, and cried; and the people wept that night.

"And all the children of Israel murmured against Moses and against Aaron: and the whole congregation said unto them, Would God that we had died in the land of Egypt! or would God we had died in this wilderness!

"And wherefore hath the Lord brought us unto this land, to fall by the sword, that our wives and our children should be a prey? were it not better for us to return into Egypt?

"And they said one to another, Let us make a captain, and let us return into Egypt.

"Then Moses and Aaron fell on their faces before all the assembly of the congregation of the children of Israel." (Numbers 14:1-5.)

Here was another demonstration of the weakness of the people, and of their complete lack of faith. After all the miracles they had witnessed, being given both food and drink by miraculous means in the wilderness; having seen the Red Sea divided to let them through; having watched the army of Pharaoh destroyed there; and having experienced the miraculous events at Sinai, they still could not fully get into their minds that they were on the Lord's journey, fulfilling his purposes, and that he would see them safely into Canaan.

How blind they were, and how faithless! It was inconceivable to Moses that they now "said one to another, Let us make a captain, and let us return into Egypt." (Numbers 14:4.)

This was rebellion. These rebels were ready to repudiate Moses, choose a new leader, reject all the Lord had done, and even return to slavery, rather than to join the assault on the well-fortified cities of Canaan.

They seemed to prefer brick-making in Egypt—hoping for its fleshpots too, of course—rather than to trust the Lord to win their battles for them. But many were strong and ready to obey the Lord in all things.

Joshua was a leader among the faithful and showed his strength and loyalty and his undeviating faith in God by standing with Caleb. They had been two of the company of scouts, and they held an entirely different opinion from the others. They were brave men, and true. They were not afraid to fight any war that the Lord commanded. Trusting in God to win their battles, they knew Canaan could be taken, and they said so.

Seeing the effect of the negative report upon the people, they rent their clothes and spoke unto all the company of the children of Israel, saying, "The land, which we passed through to search it, is an exceeding good land.

"If the Lord delight in us, then he will bring us into this land, and give it us; a land which floweth with milk and honey.

"Only rebel not ye against the Lord, neither fear ye the people of the land; for they are bread for us: their defence is departed from them, and the Lord is with us: fear them not.

"But all the congregation bade stone them with stones." (Numbers 14:7-10.)

Here was a crisis. The Lord and his prophets had brought the Israelites through their escape from slavery, through the experiences at Sinai, and protected and fed them in the wilderness; yet now, on the threshold of the Promised Land, some rebelled and refused to go.

The Lord was greatly angered. He came down and his glory appeared in the tabernacle "before all the children of Israel.

"And the Lord said unto Moses, How long will this people provoke me? and how long will it be ere they believe me, for all the signs which I have shewed among them?

"I will smite them with the pestilence, and disinherit them, and will make of thee a greater nation and mightier than they." (Numbers 14:11-12.)

Here Moses showed the greatness of his soul. He also revealed courage such as few if any men have ever shown in speaking to the Lord. He argued with the Almighty. Although the Lord had promised to make Moses' descendants into a greater nation than Israel if he destroyed the rebellious Twelve Tribes, Moses did not want that. He wanted the present congregation brought into their promised refuge.

> And Moses said unto the Lord, Then the Egyptians shall hear it, (for thou broughtest up this people in thy might from among them;)
>
> And they will tell it to the inhabitants of this land: for they have heard that thou Lord art among this people, that thou Lord art seen face to face, and that thy cloud standeth over them, and that thou goest before them, by day time in a pillar of a cloud, and in a pillar of fire by night.
>
> Now if thou shalt kill all this people as one man, then the nations which have heard the fame of thee will speak, saying,
>
> Because the Lord was not able to bring this people into the land which he sware unto them, therefore he hath slain them in the wilderness.
>
> And now, I beseech thee, let the power of my Lord be great, according as thou hast spoken, saying,
>
> The Lord is longsuffering, and of great mercy, forgiving iniquity and transgression, and by no means clearing the guilty, visiting the iniquity of the fathers upon the children unto the third and fourth generation.
>
> Pardon, I beseech thee, the iniquity of this people according unto the greatness of thy mercy, and as thou hast forgiven this people, from Egypt even until now. (Numbers 14:13-19.)

The Lord then responded according to the wish of Moses, and said:

I have pardoned according to thy word:

But as truly as I live, all the earth shall be filled with the glory of the Lord.

Because all those men which have seen my glory, and my miracles, which I did in Egypt and in the wilderness, and have tempted me now these ten times, and have not hearkened to my voice;

Surely they shall not see the land which I sware unto their fathers, neither shall any of them that provoked me see it:

But my servant Caleb, because he had another spirit with him, and hath followed me fully, him will I bring into the land whereinto he went; and his seed shall possess it. (Numbers 14:20-24.)

In his further anger the Lord said to Moses on that day:

How long shall I bear with this evil congregation, which murmur against me? I have heard the murmurings of the children of Israel, which they murmur against me.

Say unto them, As truly as I live, saith the Lord, as ye have spoken in mine ears, so will I do to you:

Your carcases shall fall in this wilderness; and all that were numbered of you, according to your whole number, from twenty years old and upward, which have murmured against me,

Doubtless ye shall not come into the land, concerning which I sware to make you dwell therein, save Caleb the son of Jephunneh, and Joshua the son of Nun.

But your little ones, which ye said should be a prey, them will I bring in, and they shall know the land which ye have despised.

But as for you, your carcases, they shall fall in this wilderness.

And your children shall wander in the wilderness forty years, and bear your whoredoms, until your carcases be wasted in the wilderness.

After the number of the days in which ye searched the land, even forty days, each day for a year, shall ye bear your iniquities, even forty years, and ye shall know my breach of promise.

I the Lord have said, I will surely do it unto all this evil congregation, that are gathered together against me: in this wilderness they shall be consumed, and there they shall die.

And the men, which Moses sent to search the land, who returned, and made all the congregation to murmur against him, by bringing up a slander upon the land,

Even those men that did bring up the evil report upon the land, died by the plague before the Lord.

But Joshua the son of Nun, and Caleb the son of Jephunneh, which were of the men that went to search the land, lived still.

And Moses told these sayings unto all the children of Israel: and the people mourned greatly. (Numbers 14:27-39.)

But despite their mourning, many did not repent. They only felt sorry for themselves. It was not long until they went back to their old practices. The Lord now was willing to wait for the rebels to die off before undertaking entry into the land.

How distressing it was both to Moses and the Lord when, under these circumstances, the Israelites eventually turned to other gods, in the face of all that the Lord and his prophet had said.

"And Israel abode in Shittim, and the people began to commit whoredom with the daughters of Moab.

"And they called the people unto the sacrifices of their gods: and the people did eat, and bowed down to their gods.

"And Israel joined himself unto Baalpeor: and the anger of the Lord was kindled against Israel." (Numbers 25:1-3.)

In discussing the fertility of the land, but the necessity of cleansing it from idolatry, the *New Analytical Bible* says:

> The land was abundantly capable of supplying the needs of the chosen people. It would have been a strange anomaly if God had placed this select race in a land, isolated and limited, that was incapable of meeting their physical wants. . . .
>
> It was a serious thing to succeed such a man as Moses. Joshua had witnessed the things that happened in the wilderness, the rebellious attitudes of the people and the remarkable leadership of Moses. It was not a simple matter to step into the place of the man whose name was to stand foremost throughout the centuries.
>
> On the other hand, he had the advantage of having before him this great man's character and example. In how many situations he could raise the question, "What would Moses have done under such circumstances?" If there was anything in the fact that it was Moses he was succeeding to cause him to hesitate, there was also everything in the fact that he had been under the leadership of Moses to steady his resolve to execute his commission in a manner pleasing to Him who had commissioned both of them.
>
> What was of greater importance was the fact that it was Jehovah who was placing in his hand this trust, and it was He who forty years before had called Moses as Israel's first great leader. To Joshua, no doubt, this was the fact of supreme significance.

It was God who called him to perform the task of settling Israel in the land. It was the highest honor. It expressed God's confidence in him, and to have such assurance of God's acceptance must outweigh all other considerations.

It was a great responsibility, but Joshua was a man of great ability. It required a man of fortitude and courage to dispossess the inhabitants of the land.

The Lord told him what he should have—courage.

He told him what he must do—to observe the Law and take the land.

He told him of what to be assured—God's constant and supporting presence and power. These are the great essentials of leadership in the Lord's work.

Idolatry in the land would be a constant, sore temptation to Israel. How essential then that at the beginning it be swept from the land. There could be no half-measures in dealing with this evil. Their pronenesss to fall into it was too much in evidence but a few days before. There was no room in Canaan for both Jehovah and Baal, and especially when the depraved heart finds Baal more alluring than Jehovah. (Chicago: John A. Dickson Publishing Co., 1941, p. 298.)

Chapter 5

THE SINS OF CANAAN

When the Lord promised the land of Canaan to Israel for a home, he described it as a land flowing with milk and honey. The scouts Moses had sent to survey the land in advance brought back contradictory accounts of the land. It was fertile and productive as the Lord said, but it was militarily strong, too.

It was also filled with moral corruption and was virtually another Sodom and Gomorrah in this respect. The people were an affront to the Lord, and their sins were as a stench arising unto heaven.

When the Lord had originally instituted the law of burnt sacrifices, he told the people that the offerings would give him a "sweet savour" as long as the people kept the commandments, but if they sinned, their "ill savour" and "stink" would come up unto the Lord. (See Joel 2:20.)

The sins of the Canaanites caused just such a stench. The Lord would tolerate them no longer. Hence he commanded Israel to put an end to it all by destroying the people. He instructed that both human and animal life should be slain and that the cities should be burned.

It will be remembered that the Promised Land at first extended from the desert to the Mediterranean Sea and from the river of Egypt to the Euphrates River. (Gen. 15:18.) Modern Israel in Palestine today is only a part of what the Lord gave to Abraham, and what remains is largely desert except where the Israelis have brought in irrigation.

But when the Twelve Tribes arrived from Egypt, Canaan was verdant and beautiful. The aridity that later came upon it was actually a part of the curse the Lord sent due to the transgression of the people.

According to tradition, the land was eventually named after Canaan, the son of Ham and grandson of Noah. This designation was first applied only to the coastal area of present-day Palestine, as indicated in Numbers 13:29 and Joshua 11:3. It afterward referred to the Jordan River valley and later still to the whole country between the Jordan and the Mediterranean. It was distinguished from the higher elevations east of the river.

Various interpretations are given to the name *Canaan.* One Bible dictionary says it means "lowland," or the Jordan valley. Another says it means "purple land" because the early inhabitants of the land made purple dyes from shellfish, which were native to that area.

Werner Keller in his splendid *The Bible as History* says that the Greeks called the manufacturers of these dyes *Phoenicians.* He says further that "Palestine comes from Pelishtim, as the Philistines are called in the Old Testament."

Keller describes the land: "Traversed by hills and mountain chains whose summits rose to over 3,000 feet, surrounded in the south and east by scrub and desert, in the north by the mountains of the Lebanon and Hermon, in the west by a flat coast with no natural harbors, it lay like a poverty-stricken island between the great kingdoms of the Nile and the Euphrates, on the frontier between two continents. East of the Nile delta, Africa stops. After a desolate stretch of 100 miles of desert Asia begins, and at its threshold lies Palestine." (New York: William Morrow and Company, 1956, p. 56.)

The dictionary in the *New Analytical Bible* defines *Canaanite* as follows:

"In particular the word denotes a descendant of Ham. In the narrower sense it applied to the people along the coast line and in the valleys (Gen. 15:21; Josh. 9:1). In the larger application of the word it included the peoples specified by Gen. 10:15-19.

"The Canaanites were the inhabitants to be driven out by Joshua (Deut. 20:17). The expulsion was not complete, and those who remained paid tribute (Judg. 1:27-36). Left in the land they became a test of the loyalty of the Israelites to Jehovah. It was not long before they fell into idolatry." (P. 80.)

Trade routes and invading armies traversed the little country, since it formed a land bridge between the valleys of the Euphrates and the Nile. It was subjected to repeated conquests by stronger neighboring nations.

Keller says that five hundred years before Abraham's day, there was a flourishing import and export trade along the Canaanite coast, with commerce involving gold, silver, ivory, painted vases, purple dyes, and cosmetics.

W. F. Albright in his *The Archaeology of Palestine* says that "the Canaanites excelled in textile manufacture, dyeing woolen cloth in rich red or blue colors with a dye prepared from a shellfish known as murex. Unfortunately no samples of cloth have survived the oxidizing agencies of 35 centuries." (Penguin Books, 1949, p. 96.)

The Canaanites were not one united nation. In fact, they were not a nation at all. They were segregated branches of their race that had settled in various parts of the land and set up independent city-states.

Jericho and Jerusalem, for example, were city-states very much like Troy and Sparta, Carthage and Rome in parallel times.

When the Israelites, therefore, invaded the land and prepared for its conquest, they had to fight each separate city and each separate king, and take the area piecemeal. This Joshua proceeded to do.

The main deity of the Canaanites was Baal, whose consort was Anath, later known as Ashtoreth, Astarte, or Diana. The religion was considered as a nature polytheism.

Its ceremonies were lascivious in the extreme. Of its human sacrifices, historians say that children were frequently used as victims in these offerings.

Baal was basically a sun god and of course his followers worshipped the sun and made offerings to it.

Ashtoreth, his consort, was the principal female divinity of the Phoenicians and was called Astarte by the Romans, Diana by the Greeks, and Ishtar by the Assyrians.

Her worship was established first in Palestine at Sidon. It will be remembered that in a later era Jezebel, the wife of the wicked King Ahab, was a Phoenician princess, and she brought Baalism into the kingdom of Israel.

Through Jezebel's daughter, Athaliah, wife of Jehoram, king of Judah, the worship of Baal was begun in that kingdom. It was against the priests of Baal that Elijah fought so valiantly at Mount Carmel, when he called down fire from heaven to consume the sacrifice.

Baalism contributed to the downfall of Solomon; he set up a sanctuary to Baal to please one of his heathen wives. *Harper's Bible Dictionary* says of the religions of Canaan:

"Canaanite fertility cults, which were more lewd and influential than any other nature cults of the Middle East, made incursions into the austere, Wilderness-born faith of Israel. Whether in crude clay altars decorated with gross goddesses, serpents, cultic doves and bulls, or in well-constructed temples, the ritual of fertility gods was rampant in the land which Israel entered. . . .

"Some of the Canaanite 'high places' were taken over by Israel and adapted to their own worship ways." (New York: Harper and Brothers, 1952, p. 89.)

It was this that got Solomon and other kings of the period into severe difficulty and led to many of the Israelites actually adopting the religion of Baal. Some of them attempted to merge Baalism and the Mosaic doctrines, in an effort to get "the best of two worlds," but corrupted themselves in doing so.

It is, therefore, fully understandable why Almighty God was so strong in his condemnation of the Canaanites and their religion and demanded the destruction of both.

Chapter 6

THE INDUSTRY OF CANAAN

Some of the Canaanites were very progressive in business, industry, and the arts. They also were adventurous seamen and roamed the Mediterranean from one end to the other. It is said that they were the original settlers of Carthage, which in later years became the archrival of Rome.

Probably the best-known inhabitants of Palestine were those who occupied the northern end of the seacoast and were known as Phoenicians. Historians trace this coastal people back as far as the 28th century B.C.

Carved on the wall of an Egyptian temple is a scene showing what is believed to be one of the world's first seagoing vessels, made by the Egyptians, returning with Phoenician prisoners. This is dated at about 2800 B.C.

James Henry Breasted, noted historian and Egyptologist, in his *Ancient Times* says that with the fall of the Egyptian Empire (after 1200 B.C.) the ships of Egypt disappeared from the Mediterranean Sea. The same fate had overtaken the fleets of the Aegeans.

> Thus the eastern Mediterranean was left unoccupied by merchant fleets, and by 1000 B.C. the Phoenician cities were taking advantage of this opportunity. Once dwellers in the desert like the Hebrews, we remember that the Phoenicians had early occupied the towns along the Syrian coast, where they became clever navigators. The Greek craftsmen were as yet quite unable to produce such wares as the Phoenician merchant offered, and hence these oriental traders did a thriving business wherever they landed.
>
> Nor did the Phoenicians stop with the Aegean world. They sought markets also in the West, and they were the discoverers of the western Mediterranean. They finally planted settlements even as far away as the Atlantic coast of Spain.
>
> Their colony of Carthage became the most important commercial

state in the western Mediterranean and the most dangerous rival of Rome. For some three centuries after 1000 B.C. they were the greatest merchants in the . . . Mediterranean world. They had no armies, however, and little political organization. The only Phoenician colony that ever became a strong state was Carthage.

The Phoenicians learned the methods of manufacturing their goods, in almost all cases, from Egypt. There they learned to make glass and porcelain, to weave linen and dye it, to cast and hammer and engrave metal. On the other hand, we find that the *designs* employed in their art were international. Their metal platters they engraved with designs which they found in both Egypt and Asia. The art of Phoenicia was thus a kind of oriental composite or combination, drawn chiefly from the Nile and the Two Rivers [Tigris and Euphrates].

We remember that it was Phoenician workmen whom the Assyrian kings employed to make furniture and metal work for the royal palace. King Solomon likewise employed Phoenician workmen to build for him the Hebrew temple at Jerusalem. After 1000 B.C. the Phoenicians were thus the artistic manufacturers of a great world extending from Nineveh on the east to Greece on the west.

On the metal platters and the furniture of carved ivory landed from the Phoenician ships, the Greek craftsmen found decorations made up of palm trees, lotus flowers, hunting scenes along the Nile, the Assyrian tree of life and many other picturesque things, but especially those strange winged creatures of oriental fancy, the sphinx, the gryphon, the winged horse. (Chicago: University of Chicago Press, n.d., pp. 266-68.)

One of the most important contributions made by the Phoenicians was their alphabet. Of this Breasted says:

The Greeks now received from the Phoenicians a priceless gift, far more valuable than all the manufactured wares of the Orient. Indeed it was the most important contribution that ever reached Europe from abroad. This new gift was an alphabet.

By 1000 B.C. the Phoenicians had long since given up the inconvenient clay tablet of Babylonia. Indeed a century before this date they were already importing great quantities of papyrus paper from Egypt. Then they devised their own system of twenty-two signs for writing their own language. It contained no signs for syllables, but each sign represented a single consonant. There were no signs for the vowels, which remained unwritten. . . .

The Phoenicians were thus the first people to devise a system of writing containing nothing but alphabetic signs; that is, true letters. This great achievement of the Phoenicians was largely due to Egyptian influence. (Ibid., p. 270.)

Breasted points out that the Phoenicians did not leave any great literature. The alphabet they devised was adopted generally by their own business people, since it was so convenient to write upon papyrus paper instead of clay tablets.

These Canaanites, known even in New Testament times as Phoenicians, traced their origin to the region of the Persian Gulf. They spoke a Semitic dialect. Their two chief cities were Tyre and Sidon. The lumber for their ships came from Lebanon, and an active commerce was conducted by the Phoenicians with all their close neighbors, as well as with nations across the sea. It was Hiram, king of Tyre, another city-state, who furnished both materials and skilled artisans to work on Solomon's temple.

Such were the Phoenicians, known to the people of Joshua as that portion of the Canaanites who lived along the seashore. Obviously the Israelites did not destroy them when they invaded the Promised Land, but lived with them side by side.

Chapter 7

The Hittite nation was one of the strongest with which the Israelites had to deal. Since the Hittites were such formidable opponents of Joshua and his people, some background concerning them should be of interest.

The Hittites were the descendants of Heth, who himself was a son of Canaan, who was a son of Ham, the son of Noah. (See Genesis 10:15.)

In the time of Abraham the descendants of Heth lived near Hebron; it was from one of them that Abraham purchased the cave of Machpelah as a tomb for his wife, Sarah. (Genesis 23.)

Esau married two Hittite women. (Genesis 26:34-35; 36:2.)

The Hittites were in the land when Moses sent spies to survey the area. (Numbers 13:29.) Uriah, with whose wife King David committed adultery, was a Hittite who fought in the armies of Israel until he was purposely led to his death by the wickedness of David.

The Hittites became one of the most powerful nations of the entire Middle East in the period of the exodus.

They lived in an area about the size of Texas, north of Palestine in Asia Minor, now Turkey. They enjoyed great prosperity in their key position in the fabled Fertile Crescent. Their valleys and plains produced abundant crops. The seaward slopes of the mountains, especially along the Black Sea, were clad with flourishing forests. The northern shores of Asia Minor, east of the Halys River, were rich in iron deposits, which allowed the Hittites to become the earliest distributors of iron when it began to displace bronze in the Mediterranean world.

The Hittites learned cuneiform writing by 2000 B.C., possibly earlier. They borrowed much from the Egyptians in the line of education and art. Due to that influence, they devised a system of writing that included picture signs and phonetic values. Historians record that with these hieroglyphic signs they engraved great stone records like those of Egypt, cut into masonry walls and on rocky cliffs.

In their business they used the two existing forms of writing, cuneiform and hieroglyphic. The hieroglyphic records carved on stone walls have not yet been deciphered. However, it is admitted that the Hittite sculptors had little skill with a chisel.

Their religion centered in the worship of the great "Earth-Mother," their chief goddess, later revered in both Crete and Greece.

At first the Hittites had various disconnected city-states, but in about 1500 B.C. the strongest unit among them built a capital city at Khatti on the east side of the Halys River. There the kings erected imposing palaces and temples and built a great wall around the city, according to the custom of that time. This city-state then succeeded in gaining control of other Hittite kingdoms and consolidated them into one powerful nation in what is now Turkey.

This empire lasted for more than two hundred years (1450-1200 B.C.). It was powerful militarily and had as its chief offensive force an army of charioteers, which contributed much to the breakdown of the Egyptian Empire.

When these people began to work the iron mines along the Black Sea and to export iron to neighboring nations, they were responsible for opening the iron age for that region. Egypt especially began to import iron from the Hittites, who sent to Ramses II, as a special gift, a large sword made of iron.

It was not the Israelites who finally overcame the Hittites. It was invasion of the Greeks and the Indo-Europeans that did that.

Breasted describes their fall in these words:

> During the thousand years between 200 and 1000 B.C. the Greeks thus took possession not only of the whole Greek peninsula but likewise of the entire Aegean world. . . .
>
> Probably before 1500 B.C. some of these invaders of Asia Minor had become so numerous among the Hittites, who were not originally Indo-Europeans, that the Hittite communities began to lose their own tongue and to speak the Indo-European language of the newcomers. Thus the Hittite cuneiform tablets are in a language which contains Indo-European words and grammatical forms akin to those in Greek, as the new decipherment has recently shown. By 1200 B.C. a second wave of Indo-Europeans, especially the Phrygians and the Armenians, were invading the Hittite country in Asia Minor.
>
> The northern Mediterranean all along its eastern end was thus being absorbed by Indo-European peoples. The result was that both the Aegeans and their Hittite neighbors in Asia Minor were overwhelmed by the advancing Indo-European line. The Hittite Empire completely collapsed. (*Ancient Times,* p. 255.)

The combined influence of India and Europe as expressed through these Indo-European invasions became permanent and important. The largest family of languages in the world consists of these Indo-European tongues, including most of the languages of Europe, India, and Southwest Asia.

The classifications include:

Germanic, made up primarily of the Germanic, Scandinavian, English, and other northern European languages.

Celtic, including Welsh, Cornish, Breton, Irish Gaelic, Scottish Gaelic, and Manx.

Italic, which included Portuguese, Spanish, Judeo-Spanish, Catalan, French, Haitian Creole, Italian, Rhaeto-Romanic, Sardinian, Dalmatian, and Romanian.

Slavic, including Russian, Ukranian, Polish, Czech, Yugoslavian, Macedonian, and Bulgarian.

Iranian. Those of Persia, Turkey, Iraq, West Pakistan, Central Asia, Afghanistan, and the Caucasus.

Indic. Those of India, Kashmir, Panjab, Bengal, Nepal, Ceylon, and related groups.

The Albanian, Greek, and Baltic languages, with those

of Latvia, Lithuania, southern Italy, and the eastern Mediterranean, were classified by themselves.

The invasion of the Indo-European tribes had an impact that remains with us today.

Chapter 8

THE PHILISTINES

The most relentless foes of the Israelites were the Philistines. According to Genesis 10:14, they were descendants of Ham through Mizraim and Casluhim "out of whom came Philistim."

They occupied the coastal area of the Promised Land south of Phoenicia. The area began at what is now the location of Bethlehem and went south to the Sinai. During the reign of David, the Philistines were crowded into a very narrow strip along the coastline.

Being bitter fighters, they cruelly afflicted Israel during her sinful days and for a time virtually enslaved the chosen race. It was with the Philistines that Samson had his difficulties when he fell in love with the treacherous Delilah.

For years little was known by historians about the Philistines—about who they were or whence they came. But archaeology recently has lifted the curtain to some extent and revealed that they were a warlike people who invaded the Palestine area about 1200 B.C. and came down toward Egypt, destroying farms and cities, burning individual homes, and killing the local inhabitants by the thousands on their way.

Reports were rushed to Egypt by swift running messengers to give warning of their approach. As they first entered the Palestine area, the Philistines attacked and crushed many Canaanitish strongholds, then rolled on like a flood toward Egypt.

Ramses III, the pharaoh at that time (1195-1164 B.C.), made hurried preparations to meet the invading horde. He strengthened his armies, manned his borders, and organized strong chariot brigades for the most effective defense.

When the invading Philistines drew near, the Egyptians attacked with the fury of lions, as their own inscriptions say. "Under the hooves of the bullocks and horses the bodies of the slain lie in heaps," one inscription reads. The Egyptians won a mighty victory, took many Philistine prisoners, and scattered their army.

There was a naval battle, too, in which the enemy attempted to seize the river delta. The Philistines had brought their own ships along and attacked the Egyptians fiercely. But the bowmen of Ramses poured down a "murderous hail of arrows upon the foreigners who provided a mass target." (Keller, p. 169.) The stricken men fell overboard.

"When the enemy had been decimated and was in complete disorder, the Egyptians rowed toward them and capsized their boats. Those who escaped death by the hail of arrows or by drowning were killed or captured by Egyptian soldiers on the nearby shore." (Ibid.) The battle took place in 1188 B.C.

Keller says that "Ramses III had been able to ward off this deadly threat to Egypt on land and sea in these two decisive battles. There had been no victory like it in all the past history of the Nile." (Ibid.)

The remaining body of Philistines returned north and settled in the area south of the Phoenicians, along the seacoast of Palestine. There they became the bane of the Israelites, the conquerers of Saul, and the worst threat to the regime of David.

The Philistines processed iron while they lived in Canaan and used it for armor, implements, and ornaments. It is believed that they learned how to smelt iron ore from the Hittites, who first produced that metal in about 1200 B.C.

When Joshua entered the Promised Land he avoided attacking the five main cities of the Philistines, but three of them, Gaza, Ashkelon, and Ekron, were later captured by Judah.

Chapter 9

THE CITIES OF CANAAN

The frightened scouts of Moses truly had seen strong cities in Canaan. For those who had no faith in the continued miracles of God, the conquest seemed like a dubious venture.

Most of the cities of Palestine in that day were built on hills for defense purposes. The cities were walled and some of the masonry fortifications, which ranged from six to fourteen feet thick, were higher than the roofs of the houses.

In his *Archaeology and the Bible*, Dr. George A. Barton, professor emeritus of Semitic languages at the University of Pennsylvania, described those cities as follows:

> The cities of Palestine were usually built on hills. These elevations, surmounted as they were by walls, created a natural means of defense from attack. Even more important than an elevated situation was a water supply, hence all Palestinian cities of importance are near springs. The necessity of being near a spring led, in some cases, to the erection of a city on a level plain. This was the case with Jericho; the only mound at its site is that created by the city itself.
>
> The hills on which the cities were erected varied in height. That at Megiddo rose to a height of but 45 to 90 feet above the surrounding land, but even this elevation was a great protection from the simple methods of attack known to ancient warfare.
>
> The hill Ophel, the site of Jebusite Jerusalem, rises today from 60 to 150 feet above the valley of the Kidron, and in ancient times that valley was from 20 to 50 feet deeper than it is now. The same hill was separated from the land on the west by a valley the bed of which in ancient times was from 50 to 100 feet below the top of the hill.
>
> The hill on which Samaria was situated rose some 300 feet above the surrounding valley on all sides except the east, and when fortified presented such an impregnable front that it took even an Assyrian army three years to capture it. (2 Kings 17:5.)

In the Seleucid and Roman periods, when some cities expanded in size, the hilltops were sometimes abandoned and they spread out over the plain. This was the case with Gerasa and Philadelphia (Rabbah Ammon). But "a city set on a hill" (Matt. 5:14) was a common feature of the Palestinian landscape. (Philadelphia: American Sunday School Union, 1925, pp. 38-40.)

Most of the cities were surrounded by heavy walls, which fortified them in case of war. Since each city was autonomous and self governing, it usually had its own king and its own soldiers.

Some walls were heavy and high; others were not. For example, at Gezer the first wall was only six feet high and two feet thick and had a sloping bank of earth packed against it on the outside.

During the Amorite period, a second wall was built at Gezer. It was thirteen feet thick; the height was equal to that of the roofs of the houses; and observation towers were placed every ninety feet along the wall. According to the historians, it was built about 2500 B.C.

As the population of the city increased and homes overflowed beyond this wall, still another wall was erected as an outer perimeter. It was fourteen feet thick and also contained towers at intervals.

The walls at Megiddo were made partly of brick and partly of rock and earth, with a stone facing. These walls also were thirteen feet thick.

Dr. Barton further describes the walls in this manner:

The kind of stones used in city walls varied with the circumstances and the degree of civilization. The walls of the stone age were naturally made of small undressed stones. The Amorites began the use of cut stone. Their blocks are often fairly smooth and regular. The Amorite wall of Gezer was made of more regular stones than the wall of the Egyptian period. In the Israelitish and Jewish periods a stone with an embossed edge was often used. It is found in the wall of Nehemiah, excavated by Bliss,—a wall made of stones that some preexilic king had used before,—and appears also in the structure of Herod the Great. . . .

The areas of Palestinian cities in the early time were very small. All of Canaanite Jericho could be put in the Colosseum at Rome! Megiddo, one of the largest of these early cities, was built on a mound that contained only about eleven acres, and Jebusite Jerusalem was built on a ridge that in ancient times contained not less than nine or more than thirteen acres. (Ibid., pp. 141-42.)

Dr. Barton described the houses in those cities, built along narrow and crooked lanes. There was little if any sanitation.

The houses were usually built of rough stones, occasionally of brick, and were set in mud. There was no evidence of mortar or cement. Usually the floors were of the plain earth. Doorways were merely openings in the walls, although occasionally wooden doors were made.

Jericho was one of the strongest and best-defended cities in the area. At the time of Joshua Jerusalem proved to be virtually impregnable, and invaders were unable to capture it. Jerusalem was not taken until the days of David.

Chapter 10

THE ROAD TO JERICHO

Jericho is less than twenty-five miles from Jerusalem. Both are on the north end of the Dead Sea, Jerusalem being in the hill country to the west, Jericho being in the Jordan River valley. Jericho was some ten miles nearer the Dead Sea than Jerusalem was.

The invading Israelites had come north through Moab and had encamped opposite Jericho, on the east side of the river. Jericho was their logical first target.

But they had to cross the river to gain access to the land. This would be hard, for the people were numerous. With their cattle, sheep, and goats, with their tents and other property, with the little children and the pregnant women, the crossing could be a major problem. How would they best negotiate it?

Boats were out of the question. They were desert people and hardly saw enough water even to drink at times. They had no equipment with which to build bridges either. (Had they ever seen a bridge?) Once again the Lord would have to provide, as he always had done, regardless of the murmurings and complaints of the people.

But before undertaking to cross the river, Joshua wanted to know more about what was on the other side of it. He and Caleb, before Moses' death, had traversed a good part of the land, but now he felt the need of more surveillance, since he had attack in mind.

The camp was at Shittim in the land of Moab. From there Joshua sent out two men to "spy secretly" and "view the land, even Jericho." This they did. (Joshua 2:1.)

The people of Jericho had observed the approach of

this vast multitude. They already had learned of their strength in war, for the Israelites had battled some of the kings and destroyed some of the cities on the other side of Jordan.

This frightened the people of Jericho, seeing that the Israelites were coming in their direction. They felt certain they would be attacked by this invading army.

When Joshua's spies entered the city, they entered the home of a woman named Rahab, seeking shelter. Seeing an opportunity to save herself, Rahab took them in.

"And she said unto the men, I know that the Lord hath given you the land, and that your terror is fallen upon us, and that all the inhabitants of the land faint because of you.

"For we have heard how the Lord dried up the water of the Red sea for you, when ye came out of Egypt; and what ye did unto the two kings of the Amorites, that were on the other side Jordan, Sihon and Og, whom ye utterly destroyed.

"And as soon as we had heard these things, our hearts did melt, neither did there remain any more courage in any man, because of you: for the Lord your God, he is God in heaven above, and in earth beneath." (Joshua 2:9-11.)

The Israelite spies had been recognized as soon as they entered the city gates, and though they were not taken at that moment, word was sent to the king, saying, "Behold, there came men in hither to night of the children of Israel to search out the country."

He was also informed that the men had entered Rahab's house.

"And the king of Jericho sent unto Rahab, saying, Bring forth the men that are come to thee, which are entered into thine house: for they be come to search out all the country.

"And the woman took the two men, and hid them, and said thus, There came men unto me, but I wist not whence they were:

"And it came to pass about the time of shutting of the gate, when it was dark, that the men went out: whither the men went I wot not: pursue after them quickly; for ye shall overtake them.

"But she had brought them up to the roof of the house, and hid them with the stalks of flax, which she had laid in order upon the roof.

"And the men pursued after them the way to Jordan unto the fords: and as soon as they which pursued after them were gone out, they shut the gate." (Joshua 2:3-7.)

When the soldiers were gone she went to the men on the roof and said, "I know that the Lord hath given you the land, and that your terror is fallen upon us, and that all the inhabitants of the land faint because of you."

Then she said:

> Now therefore, I pray you, swear unto me by the Lord, since I have shewed you kindness, that ye will also shew kindness unto my father's house, and give me a true token:
>
> And that ye will save alive my father, and my mother, and my brethren, and my sisters, and all that they have, and deliver our lives from death.
>
> And the men answered her, Our life for yours, if ye utter not this our business. And it shall be, when the Lord hath given us the land, that we will deal kindly and truly with thee.
>
> Then she let them down by a cord through the window: for her house was upon the town wall, and she dwelt upon the wall.
>
> And she said unto them, Get you to the mountain, lest the pursuers meet you; and hide yourselves there three days, until the pursuers be returned: and afterward may ye go your way.
>
> And the men said unto her, We will be blameless of this thine oath which thou hast made us swear.
>
> Behold, when we come into the land, thou shalt bind this line of scarlet thread in the window which thou didst let us down by: and thou shalt bring thy father, and thy mother, and thy brethren, and all thy father's household, home unto thee.
>
> And it shall be, that whosoever shall go out of the doors of thy house into the street, his blood shall be upon his head, and we will be guiltless: and whosoever shall be with thee in the house, his blood shall be on our head, if any hand be upon him.
>
> And if thou utter this our business, then we will be quit of thine oath which thou hast made us to swear.
>
> And she said, According unto your words, so be it. And she sent them away, and they departed: and she bound the scarlet line in the window.

And they went, and came unto the mountain, and abode there three days, until the pursuers were returned: and the pursuers sought them throughout all the way, but found them not.

So the two men returned, and descended from the mountain, and passed over, and came to Joshua the son of Nun, and told him all things that befell them:

And they said unto Joshua, Truly the Lord hath delivered into our hands all the land; for even all the inhabitants of the country do faint because of us. (Joshua 2:12-24.)

It may be wondered how the spies could have been so readily recognized as they entered Jericho. Archaeologists say that the city occupied only from six to ten acres of land. Strangers therefore were quickly noticed, since all the inhabitants of the city evidently knew each other well. The fact that the circumference of the city was so small also makes more understandable how the Israelite army could march around it so easily each day for a week.

Lying deep in the Jordan valley, Jericho was 825 feet below sea level. Jerusalem is 3,200 feet higher in elevation than Jericho. Many subtropical fruits grow near Jericho, such as dates, figs, bananas, and grapes, but also balsam, roses, henna, and the plum-like myrobalan, which was used anciently for ink.

The city is believed to date back well beyond 4000 B.C., which is merely conjecture, of course. Jericho had different sites over the centuries; the town was rebuilt on alternate but nearby locations after sieges, earthquakes, and other catastrophes. In some of the mounds, archaeologists have found as many as seven layers of houses, one on top of the other, indicating that new peoples built on the older ruins still remaining.

Ancient Jericho was surrounded by masonry and stone walls, with lookout towers at regular intervals around the structure. In places the walls were fourteen feet thick and twenty-five feet high; in other places the archaeologists indicate the walls were narrower. Their full height is not definitely known because of their eroded condition after so many centuries.

Jericho lay directly in the pathway of the invading Israelites. They needed to take Jericho before they could enter and conquer other parts of Canaan. This is what Joshua planned to do.

Chapter 11

THE JORDAN SEPARATES

Like Moses, Joshua was a man of miracles. He believed in them and taught his people to do likewise. This he accomplished by reference to demonstrated happenings they had seen and could not deny. It was one way he had of teaching them to believe in the true and living God, rather than in dumb idols.

Joshua was a prophet and a revelator, and he led his people by divine direction. He took no honor to himself. He knew that the entire migration of Israel was the Lord's doing and that he himself was simply as Moses had been—an instrument through whom the Lord worked.

It was vital that the people come to realize that God did speak through Joshua and performed miracles through him as he had done through Moses.

They were so prone to seek other gods and to forget the miracles of the true God! They were so prone to disobey, to sin through lack of faith! Joshua constantly had to remind them of the reality of things, had to warn them against the will-o-the-wisp of handmade images. After receiving the report from his scouts, Joshua said to the people: "Sanctify yourselves: for to morrow the Lord will do wonders among you." (Joshua 3:5.)

Again Joshua was teaching them that it was God who would see them over the Jordan, for they could not cross by any power of their own. Many scholars of today are in the same position as many ancient Israelites were, refusing to recognize the miracles that happened. But miracles they were, and they could not be denied.

Preparatory to the crossing, the Lord again comforted and encouraged Joshua, saying, "This day will I begin to magnify thee in the sight of all Israel, that they may know that, as I was with Moses, so I will be with thee." (Joshua 3:7.)

The Lord then instructed that the priests carrying the ark of the covenant should approach the river first. As Joshua announced this, once again he impressed on the people that the ark was that of the true and living God. When he referred to it he said, "The ark of the Lord—the Lord of all the earth." (Joshua 3:13.)

He was determined not to allow them to forget the command received on Sinai: "Thou shalt have no other gods before me." (Exodus 20:3.)

When they forgot the law, they worshipped idols. They were that fickle. It is dreadful to think of the strong attraction that idolatry really held. We hesitate to place ancient Israel among the idolatrous. But the idolatry of that day did attract many, primarily because it was a sensual religion inviting licentious practices.

The fact that sensuality was fairly extensive in Israel is evident in the divine laws against sex sin in all its varieties as set forth in Leviticus. (See chapters 18 to 21.) People with those wicked inclinations could be persuaded very easily to go after the attraction of the flesh, and to them the practices of the Canaanites may have been very enticing.

The command to cross Jordan was given when all was in readiness. The priests carrying the ark went first, as planned. As their feet entered the river the waters were shut off *from above*—not just at the site of the crossing but from above—and they stood as in a heap. (Joshua 3:8-17.)

This is interesting in view of some speculations that the crossing came in the dry season and that the stream had probably just dried up, or that a strong wind came at the convenient and appropriate time and swept the waters away from the crossing site. Why will not mankind accept the fact that God is a God of miracles? Why will they not admit that a miracle took place here as it had at the Red Sea?

Verses 15 and 16 of Joshua 3 are significant in this regard. They read:

"And as they that bare the ark were come unto Jordan, and the feet of the priests that bare the ark were dipped in the brim of the water, (*for Jordan overfloweth all his banks all the time of harvest*,)

"That the waters which came down *from above* stood and rose up upon an heap *very far from the city Adam,* that is beside Zaretan: and those that came down toward the sea of the plain, even the salt sea, *failed, and were cut off:* and the people passed over right against Jericho."

Then verse 17 says:

"And the priests that bare the ark of the covenant of the Lord stood firm on dry ground in the midst of Jordan, and all the Israelites passed over on dry ground, until all the people were passed clean over Jordan."

When the text speaks of the water being stopped *from above,* and when it mentions that it was backed up in a heap apparently as far as the vicinity of Zaretan, it is well to remember that Zaretan is a village near the town of Bethshean, near the Lake of Galilee, which is about forty miles north and *upstream* from Jericho.

The American Translation of the Bible by Smith and Goodspeed gives this version:

"When the people left their tents to cross the Jordan, with the priests carrying the ark of the covenant preceding the people, then, as soon as the bearers of the ark reached the Jordan, and the feet of the priests carrying the ark dipped in the brink of the water (the Jordan being flooded above all its banks during all the time of harvest) the waters flowing *down from above* came to a stop, rising up in a single heap, *and extending for a long distance from Adamah, a city that is in the vicinity of Zarethan;* while those flowing down toward the Sea of the Arabah, the Salt Sea [the Dead Sea] *were completely cut off,* so that the people crossed over, opposite Jericho." (Italics added.)

The Moffatt Bible makes it equally clear with this expression: "the waters that flow down stopped *and were dammed up at a distance at Adamah* (a town beside Zartan) while the waters that flow away to the sea of the Arabah (the Salt Sea) were cut off and failed" (italics added), indicating that the river had separate branches that went more directly to the sea.

The Roman Catholic "Jerusalem Bible" makes it even more clear:

"*The upper waters* stood still and made one heap over a wide space—*from Adam to the fortress of Zarethan*—while those flowing down to the Sea of Arabah, that is, the Salt Sea, stopped running altogether," again indicating auxiliary streams.

The Knox Version (Catholic) reads: "The stream above them halted its course. *Far up, all the way from the city of Adom to the place called Sarthan, these upper waters looked like a swelling mound.*" (Italics added.)

Other modern translations also sustain the account. Several considerations should be kept in mind. One is that the Israelites were crossing the river at its flood stage, and that the high water each harvest time covered an extensive area. Hence no one can say that it was the dry season and that the river simply dried up.

Neither did some casual wind come along and blow the water out of the streambed at that particular site.

The water backed up as far as the village of Adam and that is *forty miles upstream from Jericho.*

The Lord by some miracle created a type of dam that only he knew about and it held back the water; and obviously, from the scripture, the dam backed the water up for some forty miles to the town of Adam, which is near the Sea of Galilee.

It is significant that the water had been backed up so far upstream that "those that came down toward the sea," that is, the auxiliary streams that led more directly toward the Salt Sea, dried up.

It was as remarkable a miracle as was the parting of the Red Sea; though it was possibly on a smaller scale, it was of the same type. Some ridicule the Red Sea account, since they do not believe in miracles, but that crossing is sustained in the Book of Mormon, the Doctrine and Covenants, and other modern revelation. Those modern revelations and scriptures are true!

Hence we who believe in the Lord may take his revealed word, and thereby know and accept the facts. We need not be misled by the conjectures of unbelievers.

When all the people had successfully crossed the river channel on dry ground, the waters returned to their place. The Lord then commanded Joshua to set up a memorial of the event so that subsequent generations would always remember the great thing that had happened there. Twelve men were called to prepare the memorial. They took twelve stones from "the midst of Jordan" and placed them where the priests had stood while holding the ark of the covenant as the company passed by.

The scripture describes it as follows:

> Then Joshua called the twelve men, whom he had prepared of the children of Israel, out of every tribe a man:
>
> And Joshua said unto them, Pass over before the ark of the Lord your God into the midst of Jordan, and take ye up every man of you a stone upon his shoulder, according unto the number of the tribes of the children of Israel:
>
> That this may be a sign among you, that when your children ask their fathers in time to come, saying, What mean ye by these stones?
>
> Then ye shall answer them, That the waters of Jordan were cut off before the ark of the covenant of the Lord; when it passed over Jordan, the waters of Jordan were cut off: and these stones shall be for a memorial unto the children of Israel for ever.
>
> And the children of Israel did so as Joshua commanded, and took up twelve stones out of the midst of Jordan, as the Lord spake unto Joshua, according to the number of the tribes of the children of Israel, and carried them over with them unto the place where they lodged, and laid them down there.
>
> And Joshua set up twelve stones in the midst of Jordan, in the place where the feet of the priests which bare the ark of the covenant stood: and they are there unto this day. (Joshua 4:4-9.)

The river was similarly divided on two other occasions. Both were miracles, just as was the above-mentioned instance.

When Elijah and Elisha needed to cross the river together, "Elijah took his mantle, and wrapped it together, and smote the waters, and they were divided hither and thither, so that they two went over on dry ground." (2 Kings 2:8.)

Following this, Elijah was taken into heaven on the fiery chariot. As Elisha returned from this experience, he had to again cross the river to reach his home. "And he took the mantle of Elijah that fell from him, and smote the waters, and said, Where is the Lord God of Elijah? and when he also had smitten the waters, they parted hither and thither: and Elisha went over." (2 Kings 2:14.)

Under no circumstance could critics say that in these instances some convenient wind came along and blew the streambed dry, or that the two prophets walked across during a severe drouth period when the streambed was dry. These were miracles! Why not admit it?

During the forty years when the tribes traveled in the wilderness, the Lord fed them miraculously with manna. Now, on arriving in Canaan, they were able to eat "the corn of the land," which they did, making unleavened cakes and parched corn.

"And the manna ceased on the morrow after they had eaten of the old corn of the land; neither had the children of Israel manna any more; but they did eat of the fruit of the land of Canaan that year." (Joshua 5:10-12.)

Chapter 12

THE CALL TO ARMS

Forty thousand men of war were called from the ranks of Israel to attack Jericho.

The Almighty is a God of love, charity, and mercy, all of which he extends to those who serve him. But the extreme wickedness of the Canaanites was so revolting to the Lord that he could tolerate it no more. Their cup of iniquity was full. Nephi tells us that they "had rejected every word of God." (1 Nephi 17:35.) Hence the Lord used the Israelites to destroy them from before his face. They were like the people of Sodom and Gomorrah.

The Lord now sent still another sign of assurance that he would fight Israel's battles as they cleansed the land. When Joshua was near Jericho "he lifted up his eyes and looked, and, behold, there stood a man over against him with his sword drawn in his hand: and Joshua went unto him, and said unto him, Art thou for us, or for our adversaries?

"And he said, Nay; but as captain of the host of the Lord am I now come. And Joshua fell on his face to the earth, and did worship, and said unto him, What saith my lord unto his servant?

"And the captain of the Lord's host said unto Joshua, Loose thy shoe from off thy foot; for the place whereon thou standest is holy. And Joshua did so." (Joshua 5:13-15.)

Jericho was well aware of the impending attack. The city was "straitly shut up because of the children of Israel: none went out, and none came in."

The Lord then spoke to his prophet and said: "I have given into thine hand Jericho, and the king thereof, and the mighty men of valour."

What an assurance this was to Joshua, who then listened to the Lord's instruction for the battle:

"And ye shall compass the city, all ye men of war, and go round about the city once. Thus shalt thou do six days.

"And seven priests shall bear before the ark seven trumpets of rams' horns: and the seventh day ye shall compass the city seven times, and the priests shall blow with the trumpets.

"And it shall come to pass, that when they make a long blast with the ram's horn, and when ye hear the sound of the trumpet, all the people shall shout with a great shout; and the wall of the city shall fall down flat, and the people shall ascend up every man straight before him." (Joshua 6:1-5.)

In accordance with these instructions "the armed men went before the priests that blew with the trumpets, and the rereward came after the ark, the priests going on, and blowing with trumpets." (Joshua 6:9.)

Joshua instructed his men that the entire city would be smitten of the Lord, with the exception of Rahab and her family, who would be spared because she had saved the Hebrew spies when they "searched out the city."

And remembering idolatry and its seductive altars and priests, Joshua warned his people:

"And ye, in any wise keep yourselves from the accursed thing, lest ye make yourselves accursed, when ye take of the accursed thing, and make the camp of Israel a curse, and trouble it.

"But all the silver, and gold, and vessels of brass and iron are consecrated unto the Lord: they shall come into the treasury of the Lord." (Joshua 6:18-19.)

The city was encircled by the invading force of Hebrews for the full week as commanded by the Lord. Then came the climax:

"So the people shouted when the priests blew with the trumpets: and it came to pass, when the people heard the sound of the trumpet, and the people shouted with a great shout, that the wall fell down flat, so that the people went up into the city, every man straight before him, and they took the city.

"And they utterly destroyed all that was in the city, both man and woman, young and old, and ox, and sheep, and ass, with the edge of the sword." (Joshua 6:20-21.)

Joshua kept the promise of the spies to save Rahab. Before the final destruction of the city they went to her house and rescued her entire family. Then "they burnt the city with fire, and all that was therein: only the silver, and the gold, and the vessels of brass and of iron, they put into the treasury of the house of the Lord." (V. 24.)

As a final curse upon the city, Joshua said:

"Cursed be the man before the Lord, that riseth up and buildeth this city Jericho: he shall lay the foundation thereof in his firstborn, and in his youngest son shall he set up the gates of it.

"So, the Lord was with Joshua; and his fame was noised throughout all the country." (Vv. 26-27.)

Jericho was rebuilt after this destruction despite the curse. In fact, it was rebuilt many times—but it was always destroyed again, as the curse promised. It will be remembered that Jericho was mentioned in the Savior's parable of the Good Samaritan as being a city in his day. Subsequent to that time Jericho was destroyed and rebuilt again—and again.

Chapter 13

ARCHAEOLOGY IN JERICHO

Archaeologists have spent fortunes in their excavations at Jericho. Because of the biblical account of the capture of that city by the forces of Joshua, with its miraculous implications, more than ordinary interest has been associated with this project.

The archaeologists have fully determined in their own minds that an earthquake toppled the walls of the city. There is every evidence of it, they say. The Lord once again used the forces of nature to accomplish his purposes.

The *Encyclopedia Britannica* says this about Jericho:

> After its destruction by the Israelites it was, according to the biblical account, abandoned until Hiel the Bethelite established himself there in the 9th century B.C. (1 Kings xvi, 34). . . .
>
> Old Testament Jericho has been identified in the mound known as Tall as-Sultan, situated at the source of the copious spring 'Ain as-Sultan. A number of major archaeological expeditions have worked at the site, including one during 1952-58 under the leadership of Kathleen M. Kenyon, director of the British School of Archaeology in Jerusalem. . . .
>
> Little trace has been found of the 9th-century occupation attributed in the Bible to Hiel the Bethelite, but there was a considerable settlement there in the 7th century B.C., ending perhaps at the time of the second Babylonian Exile in 586 B.C. The site was then finally abandoned, and the later Jerichos grew up elsewhere.
>
> Excavations have shown, however, that Jericho had a very long history before the biblical period, and the great importance of the site is that it provides evidence of the first development of permanent settlements and therefore of the first steps toward civilization.
>
> Traces have been found of visits of Mesolithic hunters, dated by carbon-14 to c. 9000 B.C., and of a long period of settlement by their descendants, in which flimsy huts were the only habitations. . . .
>
> These first Neolithic people were succeeded in the course of the 7th millennium by a second group, characterized by more elaborate

domestic architecture, with many-roomed houses, rectilinear in plan. Their advanced culture is demonstrated by some remarkable portrait heads, modeled in plaster over human skulls. These two successive Neolithic towns of Jericho are far older than any other town so far discovered.

Thereafter the importance of Jericho declined. Newcomers in the 5th millennium brought a much more primitive way of life, and it was not until the Early Bronze Age, c. 3000 B.C., that Jericho once more became a town. Excavations have traced its history from this time continuously down to the destruction by the Israelites in the 14th century B.C. The most interesting evidence is that for the successive arrivals and culture of the Amorites and Canaanites.

Excavations in 1950-51 also revealed something of Herodian Jericho. A magnificent facade on Wadi al-Qilt, one mile south of Old Testament Jericho, is probably part of Herod's palace; and its style, completely Italian, illustrates Herod's devotion to Rome. Traces of other fine buildings can be seen in this area, which became the centre of Roman Jericho.

Jericho of the period of the crusades was on yet a third site, a mile east of the Old Testament site, and on this the modern town grew up. An insignificant village in Turkish times, it became a winter resort in the time of the British Mandate (1922). Its major expansion, however, came after its incorporation in Jordan in 1949, with the establishment in the neighbourhood of two enormous camps of Arab refugees from Israel. The town, which has been largely rebuilt, came under Israel rule in 1967. (1974 ed., 12:1002.)

The Encyclopedia Americana gives this additional information:

After passing into various hands, Jericho was acquired by Herod the Great who built a new town south of the old site and provided a hippodrome, amphitheater, and palace. This city was destroyed by the Arabs and Persians and another Jericho was built by the Crusaders on the site where it now stands. With the departure of the Europeans, its importance declined until recently.

The modern village is on the road from Jerusalem to Amman in an agricultural area made fertile by "Elisha's Fountain," a powerful spring located on the west side of Tell es Sultan. Often visited by tourists, it has two hotels, a Greek and a Latin church, and a Russian monastery. In 1950, excavations west of the village uncovered the remains of a Hellenic fortress from the 2nd century B.C. as well as the site of the city built by Herod.

Jericho became part of the British Mandate of Palestine in 1920 and after the Israel-Arab War (1949-1949), it was included in the Hashemite Kingdom of Jordan. Pop. (1961) of the sub-district, 64,220; of the village, 10,441. (New York: Americana Corp., 1977, 16:26.)

Harper's Bible Dictionary gives this information concerning the city as restored by King Herod:

The city, some of whose buildings were of concrete faced with diamond-shaped stones and brilliantly colored plaster, was patterned after architecture characteristic of Rome from c. 80 B.C. to the death of Augustus Caesar (A.D. 14). One of the early finds was a Hellenistic fortress whose walls were square on the outer reaches and circular on the inner ones.

Along the banks of the wadi were a promenade and sunken garden, as well as a circular theater and terraced area. An imposing grand staircase led to the upper levels of hillside Jericho near a large government building.

The study of the palace of Herod the Great sheds light on a type of architecture of which little was previously known. The city continued to flourish until the end of the 1st three Christian centuries; then it gradually disappeared until Arabs in the 8th century converted it into a military outpost....

Seventeen culture levels, going down through 80 ft. of debris, have been examined at Jericho. Every year of Garstang's explorations his wife washed thousands of bits of pottery. The site yielded hints concerning the religion that prevailed there before the Hebrews came. Statuettes of triads of gods—father, mother, son—dating from the 6th millennium B.C. were found, objects evidently worshipped at a Jericho shrine.

Jericho has also yielded light on the Hyksos occupation of Egypt. The scarabs of her cemetery offer interesting historical material. A site (Teleilat el-Ghassul) near Jericho has supplied the name "Ghassulian" to the Early Chalcolithic Age (c. 4500-3000 B.C.), whose relics are found elsewhere in Palestine.

The oldest known permanent houses were found at Jericho, dating from the Neolithic or New Stone Age (in Palestine, 8000-4500 B.C.) before the art of pottery was invented; with floors of lime-surfaced, painted, and burnished clay.

Sometimes the floors of seven successive houses have been found, one below the other, with walls of adobe or beaten clay.

Albright tells of one house of early Neolithic times that had had a post-supported porch, a spacious antechamber, and a larger inner room. The occupants left no pottery, but did leave cones and other ritualistic objects.

Stratum X yielded an artist's studio, with some of its works of art still where the fashioner left them some 7,000 years ago, even before the Chalcolithic settlement at Teleilat el-Ghassul was making its brilliant frescoes. (New York: Harper and Brothers, 1952.)

Chapter 14

THE ACCURSED THING

The victory at Jericho was not without its disappointment and tragedy.

The Lord had commanded Joshua to completely destroy the city, except that the silver and gold and the vessels of brass and iron were to be placed in the Lord's house. The individual Israelites were to take no spoil.

One of the men, Achan by name, of the tribe of Judah, disobeyed. It was not discovered until the Israelite soldiers attacked the town of Ai and were bitterly defeated.

Joshua was stunned by the defeat, and fell upon the earth before the ark of the covenant seeking to know why the Lord had not won the battle for them.

"And the Lord said unto Joshua, Get thee up; wherefore liest thou thus upon thy face?

"Israel hath sinned, and they have also transgressed my covenant which I commanded them: for they have even taken of the accursed thing, and have also stolen, and dissembled also, and they have put it even among their own stuff.

"Therefore the children of Israel could not stand before their enemies, but turned their backs before their enemies, because they were accursed: neither will I be with you any more, except ye destroy the accursed from among you.

"Up, sanctify the people, and say, Sanctify yourselves against to morrow: for thus saith the Lord God of Israel, There is an accursed thing in the midst of thee, O Israel: thou canst not stand before thine enemies, until ye take away the accursed thing from among you." (Joshua 7:10-13.)

Joshua determined to conduct a tribe by tribe, man by man, search for the guilty party. When at last they came to Achan, Joshua said to him:

"My son, give, I pray thee, glory to the Lord God of Israel, and make confession unto him; and tell me now what thou hast done; hide it not from me.

"And Achan answered Joshua, and said, Indeed I have sinned against the Lord God of Israel, and thus and thus have I done:

"When I saw among the spoils a goodly Babylonish garment, and two hundred shekels of silver, and a wedge of gold of fifty shekels weight, then I coveted them, and took them; and, behold, they are hid in the earth in the midst of my tent, and the silver under it.

"So Joshua sent messengers, and they ran unto the tent; and, behold, it was hid in his tent, and the silver under it.

"And they took them out of the midst of the tent, and brought them unto Joshua, and unto all the children of Israel, and laid them out before the Lord." (Joshua 7:19-23.)

When Achan was made to face the loot, Joshua said to him:

"Why hast thou troubled us? the Lord shall trouble thee this day. And all Israel stoned him with stones. . . .

"And they raised over him a great heap of stones unto this day. So the Lord turned from the fierceness of his anger. Wherefore the name of that place was called, The valley of Achor, unto this day." (Vv. 25-26.)

Following Achan's death, Joshua determined to go up against the city of Ai once again. He sought the Lord's help, which was freely given now, and the city was taken and the king hanged.

But it was a sore lesson in obedience for Israel.

Chapter 15

THE SUN STANDS STILL

The king of Jerusalem feared Joshua. He had three reasons to be frightened.

One was that he had heard of the fate of Jericho and didn't want that to happen to him. Another was that word came of the complete destruction of Ai at the hands of the Israelites.

The third was that his neighboring kingdom of the Gibeonites had made a treaty with Joshua in an effort to save their own lives.

"That they feared greatly," says the scripture, "because Gibeon was a great city, as one of the royal cities, and because it was greater than Ai, and all the men thereof were mighty." (Joshua 10:2.)

Being a "royal city," Gibeon was a member of an alliance in which Jerusalem and other cities were involved. For the Gibeonites to treat with Israel seemed to the king of Jerusalem like an act of treason, and he was determined to punish them.

The Gibeonites' peace with Israel came by deceiving them, but when the guilt was discovered, instead of slaying the people of that kingdom, Joshua decided to enslave them and make of them "hewers of wood and drawers of water" for the congregation and the altar.

Later this treaty was broken by King Saul, who slew the Gibeonites. (2 Samuel 21.)

In fright the king of Jerusalem sent to four other kings, including the ruler of Lachish, asking them to join their armies in a battle against the Gibeonites. Once the Gibeonites were out of the way they could turn on the Israelites. This they agreed to, "and went up, they and all their hosts, and encamped before Gibeon, and made war against it." (Joshua 10:1-5.)

The Gibeonites immediately turned to Joshua for assistance and sent a message saying, "Come up to us quickly, and save us, and help us: for all the kings of the Amorites that dwell in the mountains are gathered together against us.

"So Joshua ascended from Gilgal, he, and all the people of war with him, and all the mighty men of valour.

"And the Lord said unto Joshua, Fear them not: for I have delivered them into thine hand; there shall not a man of them stand before thee."

With this, the Israelites left their tents and battled against the five kings. "And the Lord discomfited them before Israel, and slew them with a great slaughter at Gibeon, and chased them along the way that goeth up to Bethhoron, and smote them to Azekah, and unto Makkedah.

"And it came to pass, as they fled from before Israel, and were in the going down to Bethhoron, that the Lord cast down great stones from heaven upon them unto Azekah, and they died: they were more which died with hailstones than they whom the children of Israel slew with the sword." (Joshua 10:6-11.)

But the day was not long enough for the Israelites to complete their task. They needed extra hours before the sun went down.

"Then spake Joshua to the Lord in the day when the Lord delivered up the Amorites before the children of Israel, and he said in the sight of Israel, Sun, stand thou still upon Gibeon; and thou, Moon, in the valley of Ajalon.

"And the sun stood still, and the moon stayed, until the people had avenged themselves upon their enemies. Is not this written in the book of Jasher? So the sun stood still in the midst of heaven, and hasted not to go down about a whole day.

"And there was no day like that before it or after it,

that the Lord hearkened unto the voice of a man: for the Lord fought for Israel." (Joshua 10:12-14.)

The account of the sun and moon being stayed in the heavens at the request of Joshua has, of course, raised the criticism of the intellectuals. Impossible, they said; a myth, others declared. But was it?

Let us keep in mind that God declared: "Fear them not: for I have delivered them into thine hand." And he said that none could stand before Israel's hosts, as they obeyed the Lord, for the Lord would assure their victory.

It is well to remember once again that the entire history of Israel for this period was one of miracle after miracle.

The victories of Joshua were but additional miracles, for Israel was not equipped for war as the Canaanites were; they had no battering rams with which to knock down the gates and walls of the fortified cities. And their general was over eighty years old!

Commanding the sun and moon to stand still was just another episode in this series of divine acts. Impossible, some say? Is anything too hard for the Lord? (Genesis 18:14.) Was not the Lord the Creator of the sun and moon and all other heavenly bodies? Are not the laws of nature that control the earth his laws?

Other and more modern translations of the Bible support the account in the King James Version.

The Jerusalem Bible (Roman Catholic) on this point reads:

> "Sun, stand still over Gibeon,
> and, moon, you also, over the Vale of Aijalon.
> And the sun stood still, and the moon halted,
> till the people had vengeance on their enemies."

It then continues: "Is this not written in the book of the Just? The sun stood still in the middle of the sky and delayed its setting for almost a whole day. There was never a day like that before or since, when Yahweh obeyed the voice of a man, for Yahweh was fighting for Israel."

It was part of the Lord's strategy in "fighting for Israel."

The Moffatt version on this point reads:

"O Sun, stand over Gibeon
Move not, O moon, from Ajalon vale.
The sun stood still, the moon moved not
'till the folks had taken vengeance on their foes."

And then this text continues:

"Is not this written in the Book of Heroes? The sun stood still in the middle of the sky and never hastened to set for about a whole day. Never was there a day like that, before or since, when the Eternal listened to the cry of a man, for the Eternal was fighting for Israel."

Again it is seen from the scripture that it was part of the Lord's method of winning the war. It will be remembered that earlier he had rained down brimstone from heaven as he aided the Israelites in their defeat of the five kings, and the destruction from the Lord's downpour of stones was greater than that by Israel's army. (Joshua 10:11.)

It is another case of God being a God of miracles, a thing we must learn to admit.

The *New Analytical Bible* says this in connection with the miracle of the sun and moon standing still:

"At Beth-horon, Gibeon and Ajalon they were made to see in a more striking manner that the Lord was not limited in His resources, that He could put in action the forces of the universe to accomplish His will.

"Many times in Egypt and the wilderness they witnessed His miraculous power, and now the sun and moon obey His will in a manner that was calculated to stir them to the depths. It would strike fear to the hearts of the enemy, these worshipers of the Sun, to realize that their god was but an instrument in the hands of Israel's Jehovah in support of His people." (Page 299.)

The Book of Mormon helps us to understand the matter of the lengthened day as we read in the book of Helaman:

O how great is the nothingness of the children of men; yea, even they are less than the dust of the earth.

For behold, the dust of the earth moveth hither and thither, to the dividing asunder, at the command of our great and everlasting God.

Yea, behold at his voice do the hills and the mountains tremble and quake.

And by the power of his voice they are broken up, and become smooth, yea, even like unto a valley.

Yea, by the power of his voice doth the whole earth shake;

Yea, by the power of his voice, do the foundations rock, even to the very center.

Yea, and if he say unto the earth—Move—it is moved.

Yea, if he say unto the earth—Thou shalt go back, that it lengthen out the day for many hours—it is done;

And thus, according to his word the earth goeth back, and it appeareth unto man that the sun standeth still; yea, and behold, this is so; for surely it is the earth that moveth and not the sun.

And behold, also, if he say unto the waters of the great deep—Be thou dried up—it is done.

Behold, if he say unto this mountain—Be thou raised up, and come over and fall upon that city, that it be buried up—behold it is done. (Helaman 12:7-17.)

So here we have the words of a Book of Mormon prophet confirming the fact that God can—and would, when necessary—cause that the earth should stop in its rotation to lengthen a day. And since on the occasion in question he was fighting to bring victory to Israel, this was one of his means of doing so.

If we have doubts about the Lord's willingness or ability to interrupt the usual movements of heavenly bodies, how shall we explain such phenomena as the following:

"But, behold, I say unto you that before this great day shall come the sun shall be darkened, and the moon shall be turned into blood, and the stars shall fall from heaven, and there shall be greater signs in heaven above and in the earth beneath." (D&C 29:14.)

Or: "And they shall see signs and wonders, for they shall be shown forth in the heavens above and in the earth beneath. And they shall behold blood, and fire, and vapors of smoke. And before the day of the Lord shall come, the sun shall be darkened, and the moon be turned into blood, and the stars fall from heaven." (D&C 45:40-42.)

"For not many days hence and the earth shall tremble and reel to and fro as a drunken man; and the sun shall hide his face, and shall refuse to give light; and the moon shall be bathed in blood; and the stars shall become exceedingly angry, and shall cast themselves down as a fig that falleth from off a fig-tree." (D&C 88:87.)

Or: "And so great shall be the glory of his presence that the sun shall hide his face in shame, and the moon shall withhold its light, and the stars shall be hurled from their places." (D&C 133:49.)

The episode of Joshua commanding the sun and moon to stand still was insignificant compared to the stellar upsets that will accompany the second advent of the Savior, when stars will be hurled from their places. Some power will darken the sun and make the moon refuse to give its light. (Of course the moon will be darkened as soon as the sun gives no further light, since the moon's light is merely reflected from the sun.)

It is appropriate here to quote Sir Charles Marston, a most intelligent "critic of the critics," who said that it is time we begin "to recognize the extravagance of its [criticism by the intellectuals] underlying assumption, that *what the critic did not know could not have been!*" (*The Bible Comes Alive,* New York: Fleming H. Revell Company, 1947, p. 182.)

Chapter 16

THE HOLY CITY

Joshua never did besiege Jerusalem. Why he did not take it after having destroyed much of the Amorite army is not explained. The city was not conquered until the time of David.

It is a very ancient city. It was the Salem of which Melchizedek was king in Abraham's day.

The *Archaeological Encyclopedia of the Holy Land* says:

> The name is made up of two words: the root yrw, meaning "to lay a foundation," plus the name of the West Semitic (Amorite) god Shalmanu or Shalem. Although prehistoric remains from the Palaeolithic period onwards have been found in the area round the city, the first settlement on the site seems to belong to the Early Bronze Age, the great foundation era of cities in Canaan: the Amorite name also belongs to this period.
>
> Jerusalem is first mentioned in the Execration Texts as u-r-s-m-m. From that time onwards its existence is documented in literary sources as well as by archaeological remains.
>
> The site chosen for the establishment of the city lay slightly to the east of the north-south watershed of Canaan. The decisive element in its selection was the existence of a spring called Gihon that gushed out on the eastern flank of a low hill, the southernmost spur of a long narrow ridge that jutted out from the watershed.
>
> The site was very suitable for defence under conditions of ancient warfare: deep declivities (the valleys of Kidron and Hinnom) protected it from the east and west, while the sharp end of the spur protected it on the south. Only in the north was the hill connected with another elevation. The founders selected a narrow neck in the ridge for the north wall of their city.
>
> Jerusalem appears in history for the first time in the Middle Bronze Age (the period of the Patriarchs). It was then a fairly substantial city, ruled by a king called Puti-hiba in the El Amarna letters. The local aristocracy seems to have included Hittite and other Indo-Aryan elements.
>
> Slightly different local origins are suggested by the story in

Genesis (14) about the encounter of Abraham with Melchizedek, the priest-king of Salem (Jerusalem).

The reappearance of a similar theophoric suffix (one containing the name of God) in the name of Adonizedek, King of Jerusalem in the time of Joshua (Josh. 10:1), suggests that all names ending in -zedek were priestly throne names, adopted by generations of kings who were also priests of the El Elyon.

This was a Canaanite deity who was—in the normal Semitic usage—the 'owner' (baal) of the city, with the king as his nominal viceroy. From the El Amarna letters we learn that the king of Jerusalem was attempting to extend his suzerainty over other cities, while protesting his loyalty to Pharaoh and fending off the nomadic Habiru, (Hebrews) or at least pretending to do so. [Avraham Negev, ed., Weidenfeld and Nicholson, 1972, p. 166.]

Jerusalem is inland from the Mediterranean Sea about 35 miles; its altitude is 2,439 feet above sea level.

The account of Melchizedek's remarkable experience as king of Salem, included in the Book of Mormon records, is most interesting. Alma tells us:

And now, my brethren, I would that ye should humble yourselves before God, and bring forth fruit meet for repentance, that ye may also enter into that rest.

Yea, humble yourselves even as the people in the day of Melchizedek, who was also a high priest after this same order which I have spoken, who also took upon him the high priesthood forever.

And it was this same Melchizedek to whom Abraham paid tithes; yea, even our father Abraham paid tithes of one-tenth part of all he possessed.

Now these ordinances were given after this manner, that thereby the people might look forward on the Son of God, it being a type of his order, or it being his order, and this that they might look forward to him for a remission of their sins, that they might enter into the rest of the Lord.

Now this Melchizedek was a king over the land of Salem; and his people had waxed strong in iniquity and abomination; yea, they had all gone astray; they were full of all manner of wickedness;

But Melchizedek having exercised mighty faith, and received the office of the high priesthood according to the holy order of God, did preach repentance unto his people. And behold, they did repent; and Melchizedek did establish peace in the land in his days; therefore he was called the prince of peace, for he was the king of Salem; and he did reign under his father.

Now, there were many before him, and also there were many afterwards, but none were greater; therefore, of him they have more particularly made mention. (Alma 13:13-19.)

The Lord explained in a revelation to the Prophet Joseph Smith that Melchizedek received the priesthood through the lineage of the fathers even to Noah; Abraham was ordained to the priesthood by this same Melchizedek. (D&C 84:14.)

Genesis speaks of Melchizedek as follows:

"And Melchizedek king of Salem brought forth bread and wine: and he was the priest of the most high God.

"And he blessed him, and said, Blessed be Abram of the most high God, possessor of heaven and earth:

"And blessed be the most high God, which hath delivered thine enemies into thy hand. And he gave him tithes of all." (Genesis 14:18-20.)

In the 76th Psalm we have this reference to Jerusalem:

"In Judah is God known: his name is great in Israel. In Salem also is his tabernacle, and his dwelling place in Zion." (Vv. 1-2.)

In his epistle to the Hebrews Paul speaks of Melchizedek (5:10; 6:20; 7:1-17) as being without father or mother, but of course Latter-day Saints know that he was speaking of the priesthood, and not of the man.

In the discussion on priesthood in section 107 of the Doctrine and Covenants, we have this explanation:

"There are, in the church, two priesthoods, namely, the Melchizedek and Aaronic, including the Levitical Priesthood.

"Why the first is called the Melchizedek Priesthood is because Melchizedek was such a great high priest.

"Before his day it was called the *Holy Priesthood, after the Order of the Son of God.*

"But out of respect or reverence to the name of the Supreme Being, to avoid the too frequent repetition of his name, they, the church, in ancient days, called that priesthood after Melchizedek, or the Melchizedek Priesthood."

In further explaining the priesthood, the revelation goes on to say:

"The Melchizedek Priesthood holds the right of presidency, and has power and authority over all the offices in the church in all ages of the world, to administer in spiritual things.

"The Presidency of the High Priesthood, after the order of Melchizedek, have a right to officiate in all the offices in the church.

"High priests after the order of the Melchizedek Priesthood have a right to officiate in their own standing, under the direction of the presidency, in administering spiritual things, and also in the office of an elder, priest (of the Levitical order), teacher, deacon, and member. . . .

"The power and authority of the higher, or Melchizedek Priesthood, is to hold the keys of all the spiritual blessings of the church—

"To have the privilege of receiving the mysteries of the kingdom of heaven, to have the heavens opened unto them, to commune with the general assembly and church of the Firstborn, and to enjoy the communion and presence of God the Father, and Jesus the mediator of the new covenant." (Vv. 1-4; 8-10; 18-19.)

Jerusalem had a stormy history, even from the days of the patriarchs. David, of course, declared it his capital once the city was captured, and Solomon made it world famous by building the magnificent temple there.

Jerusalem was attacked and conquered at various periods. In the days of Zedekiah, king of Judah, the city was taken and the Jews were sent as captives to Babylon. This involved Lehi in about A.D. 600.

The most tragic conquest of all was that by the Romans in A.D. 70, when the Jews sought to throw off Roman government. It was then that the temple was destroyed as the Savior had predicted. (Matthew 24:1-2.)

The church of Jesus Christ centered in Jerusalem until that siege of A.D. 70. Then the Saints scattered. A number of them went to Ephesus in what is now Turkey; there, among the ruins of the once fabulous city, one can still see evidences of Christian worship including baptismal fonts in the remains of churches, fonts obviously built for baptism by immersion.

Of course the most important thing about Jerusalem was that the Savior spent so much time there, carrying on an active ministry during the three years he labored.

In Jerusalem he visited the temple when twelve years old; he later cleansed it of all bartering. He held the Last Supper in Jerusalem, and washed the feet of the disciples in an upper room there.

In Gethsemane, while bowed in prayer, he so suffered that he literally sweat blood. His agony is best described in his own words:

"For behold, I, God, have suffered these things for all, that they might not suffer if they would repent;

"But if they would not repent they must suffer even as I;

"Which suffering caused myself, even God, the greatest of all, to tremble because of pain, and to bleed at every pore, and to suffer both body and spirit—and would that I might not drink the bitter cup, and shrink—

"Nevertheless, glory be to the Father, and I partook and finished my preparations unto the children of men." (D&C 19:16-19.)

It was in Jerusalem that he was arrested; there he faced the high priest, then Pilate, then was scourged, mocked; and there—before Pilate and his enemies—he acknowledged that he was the Son of God.

It was in Jerusalem that he was condemned to die as the mobs cried out, "Crucify him, crucify him," and dreadfully agreed that his blood should be upon their own heads!

He carried his cross, but collapsed under it. He was taken to Calvary, nailed on the cross, and while dying was again insulted by the bloodthirsty mobs who had sought his life from the beginning of his ministry. He surely was despised and rejected of men; he bore our griefs and carried our sorrows; he was wounded for our transgressions; he was numbered with the transgressors but made intercession for sinners. (Isaiah 53.)

He died there, on the cross, but on the third day was resurrected, that we also might be raised from the dead.

These were the greatest events in the long history of the city. Although rejected there, he pleaded to the end for the people to repent. His words can never be forgotten:

"O Jerusalem, Jerusalem, thou that killest the prophets, and stonest them which are sent unto thee, how often would I have gathered thy children together, even as a hen gathereth her chickens under her wings, and ye would not!

"Behold, your house is left unto you desolate." (Matthew 23:37-38.)

Nephi had said that the people of that day were the most wicked on earth, the only ones evil enough to crucify their king. His words are chilling:

"Wherefore, as I said unto you, it must needs be expedient that Christ—for in the last night the angel spake unto me that this should be his name—should come among the Jews, among those who are the more wicked part of the world; and they shall crucify him—for thus it behooveth our God, and there is none other nation on earth that would crucify their God.

"For should the mighty miracles be wrought among other nations they would repent, and know that he be their God.

"But because of priestcrafts and iniquities, they at Jerusalem will stiffen their necks against him, that he be crucified.

"Wherefore, because of their iniquities, destructions, famines, pestilences, and bloodshed shall come upon them; and they who shall not be destroyed shall be scattered among all nations." (2 Nephi 10:3-6.)

This is made even more dreadful when we recall the words of the Lord to Enoch:

"Wherefore, I can stretch forth mine hands and hold all the creations which I have made; and mine eye can pierce them also, and among all the workmanship of mine hands there has not been so great wickedness as among thy brethren." (Moses 7:36.)

The evidence suggests that after the dispersion in A.D. 70, Christians stayed away from Jerusalem for 200 years. However, in the year 381 the Catholic Church held a council there, in which amendments to the Nicene Creed were suggested.

It is now an interdenominational city, the focal point of the three great religions of the world, Christian, Mohammedan, and Jewish.

Chapter 17

ANOTHER ALLIANCE CRUSHED

The destruction of the army of the Amorites and the execution of the five kings, including the ruler of Jerusalem, had wide repercussions and brought on another severe battle.

Jabin, king of Hazor, on hearing of these things, called together an imposing group of rulers in the valleys and mountains of his area, inviting them to form a military alliance against Israel. These kings came from "the north of the mountains, and of the plains south of Chinneroth, and in the valley, and in the borders of Dor on the west."

Jabin also went to the Canaanites on both the east and the west of Hazor; to the Amorites, the Hittites, the Perizzites, and the Jebusites in the mountains; and to the Hivites near Mt. Hermon.

When these kings had assembled their armies into one great force, "they came and pitched together at the waters of Merom, to fight against Israel.

"And the Lord said unto Joshua, Be not afraid because of them: for to morrow about this time will I deliver them up all slain before Israel: thou shalt hough their horses, and burn their chariots with fire.

"So Joshua came, and all the people of war with him, against them by the waters of Merom suddenly; and they fell upon them.

"And the Lord delivered them into the hand of Israel, who smote them, and chased them unto great Zidon, and unto Misrephothmaim, and unto the valley of Mizpeh eastward; and they smote them, until they left them none remaining.

"And Joshua did unto them as the Lord bade him: he

houghed their horses, and burnt their chariots with fire." (Joshua 11:1-9.)

But Joshua was not willing to leave Hazor unpunished:

"And Joshua at that time turned back, and took Hazor, and smote the king thereof with the sword: for Hazor beforetime was the head of all those kingdoms.

"And they smote all the souls that were therein with the edge of the sword, utterly destroying them: there was not any left to breathe: and he burnt Hazor with fire.

"And all the cities of those kings, and all the kings of them, did Joshua take, and smote them with the edge of the sword, and he utterly destroyed them, as Moses the servant of the Lord commanded.

"But as for the cities that stood still in their strength, Israel burned none of them, save Hazor only; that did Joshua burn.

"And all the spoil of these cities, and the cattle, the children of Israel took for a prey unto themselves; but every man they smote with the edge of the sword, until they had destroyed them, neither left they any to breathe." (Vv. 10-14.)

Here again we gain insight into the basic strength of Joshua: "He left nothing undone of all that the Lord commanded." (Joshua 11:15.)

The scripture in describing the further conquests of Joshua says this:

> So Joshua took all that land, the hills, and all the south country, and all the land of Goshen, and the valley, and the plain, and the mountain of Israel, and the valley of the same;
>
> Even from the mount Halak, that goeth up to Seir, even unto Baalgad in the valley of Lebanon under mount Hermon: and all their kings he took, and smote them, and slew them.
>
> Joshua made war a long time with all those kings.
>
> There was not a city that made peace with the children of Israel, save the Hivites the inhabitants of Gibeon: all other they took in battle.
>
> For it was of the Lord to harden their hearts, that they should come against Israel in battle, that he might destroy them utterly, and

that they might have no favour, but that he might destroy them, as the Lord commanded Moses.

And at that time came Joshua, and cut off the Anakims from the mountains, from Hebron, from Debir, from Anab, and from all the mountains of Judah, and from all the mountains of Israel: Joshua destroyed them utterly with their cities.

There was none of the Anakims left in the land of the children of Israel: only in Gaza, in Gath, and in Ashdod, there remained.

So Joshua took the whole land, according to all that the Lord said unto Moses; and Joshua gave it for an inheritance unto Israel according to their divisions by their tribes. And the land rested from war. (Joshua 11:16-23.)

Altogether Joshua conquered thirty-one kings.

However, there was still much of the land that was not conquered. Some was left alone, as in the case of Jerusalem, while other areas were merely put under tribute and were not destroyed. For instance, the tribe of Manasseh failed in its attack on cities that had been assigned to it. Says the scripture:

"Southward it was Ephraim's, and northward it was Manasseh's, and the sea is his border; and they met together in Asher on the north, and in Issachar on the east.

"And Manasseh had in Issachar and in Asher Beth-shean and her towns, and Ibleam and her towns, and the inhabitants of Dor and her towns, and the inhabitants of Endor and her towns, and the inhabitants of Taanach and her towns, and the inhabitants of Megiddo and her towns, even three countries.

"Yet the children of Manasseh could not drive out the inhabitants of those cities; but the Canaanites would dwell in that land.

"Yet it came to pass, when the children of Israel were waxen strong, that they put the Canaanites to tribute; but did not utterly drive them out." (Joshua 17:10-13.)

Chapter 18

DIVIDING THE LAND

Possessing the land of promise was the major reason for Israel's journey to Canaan. Now, having conquered thirty-one city-states or kingdoms, Joshua was ready for distribution of the property among the tribes. In general, the divisions were made as follows:

1. East of the Jordan was given to Reuben, Gad, and half the tribe of Manasseh.
2. West of the Jordan: (a) Southern section—Simeon, Benjamin, Dan, and Judah. (b) Hebron area—Caleb's special inheritance. (c) Central section—Ephraim, half the tribe of Manasseh, and Issachar; and a special inheritance for Joshua. (d) Northern section—Zebulun, Asher, and Naphtali.
3. Cities of refuge were established. On the east bank they were Bezer, Ramoth, and Golan. On the west bank there were Kadesh, Shechem, and Hebron.
4. Shiloh was declared the religious center.

The tribe of Levi received no portion of the land. They were allotted forty-eight cities for their families.

As is indicated above, Joshua was given a special inheritance in recognition of his great leadership.

In connection with the assignment of Judah's allotment of land, we have the following from the dictionary portion of the *New Analytical Bible:*

> As we look back we can see the Divine wisdom in placing this tribe in the section in which Jerusalem lay that was to play such an important part in the Messianic history of Israel. This was not realized until the time of David whose great work was to secure national centralization, and later Solomon who was to bring the nation to religious centralization in the erection of the Temple. For these things of such vital significance to Israel and the world, provision was made

under the direction of Jehovah in locating the tribe that should bring forth the Messiah.

Thus we see how much was involved in this first stage of Israel's national career under the leadership of Joshua. A nation was born by which God's gracious promises to Adam's race were to be fulfilled and through whom He is to reveal Himself to the world. The great truths of this period are the heritage of all time, and as we stand in the midst of the history of this book we realize that the lessons are for us and for every age as well as for them. (P. 299.)

The cities of refuge were most interesting. They were established by the direct revelation of the Lord:

> The Lord also spake unto Joshua, saying,
>
> Speak to the children of Israel, saying, Appoint out for you cities of refuge, whereof I spake unto you by the hand of Moses:
>
> That the slayer that killeth any person unawares and unwittingly may flee thither: and they shall be your refuge from the avenger of blood.
>
> And when he that doth flee unto one of those cities shall stand at the entering of the gate of the city, and shall declare his cause in the ears of the elders of that city, they shall take him into the city unto them, and give him a place, that he may dwell among them.
>
> And if the avenger of blood pursue after him, then they shall not deliver the slayer up into his hand; because he smote his neighbour unwittingly, and hated him not beforetime.
>
> And he shall dwell in that city, until he stand before the congregation for judgment, and until the death of the high priest that shall be in those days: then shall the slayer return, and come unto his own city, and unto his own house, unto the city from whence he fled.
>
> And they appointed Kedesh in Galilee in mount Naphtali, and Shechem in mount Ephraim, and Kirjatharba, which is Hebron, in the mountain of Judah.
>
> And on the other side Jordan by Jericho eastward, they assigned Bezer in the wilderness upon the plain out of the tribe of Reuben, and Ramoth in Gilead out of the tribe of Gad, and Golan in Bashan out of the tribe of Manasseh.
>
> These were the cities appointed for all the children of Israel, and for the stranger that sojourneth among them, that whosoever killeth any person at unawares might flee thither, and not die by the hand of the avenger of blood, until he stood before the congregation. (Joshua 20:1-9.)

The Levites were given scattered cities rather than one district to facilitate their service to the various tribes and to provide convenient locations for their families while the priests carried on their ministerial duties. With so many cities being thus designated, they were evenly distributed throughout the land. The assignment came about in this manner:

"Then came near the heads of the fathers of the Levites unto Eleazar the priest, and unto Joshua the son of Nun, and unto the heads of the fathers of the tribes of the children of Israel;

"And they spake unto them at Shiloh in the land of Canaan, saying, The Lord commanded by the hand of Moses to give us cities to dwell in, with the suburbs thereof for our cattle.

"And the children of Israel gave unto the Levites out of their inheritance, at the commandment of the Lord, these cities and their suburbs." (Joshua 21:1-3.)

Ephraim and Manasseh were given inheritances in the land of Palestine, as were the other tribes. But they were given more—in America.

It will be remembered that when Jacob blessed his sons he said to Joseph:

> Joseph is a fruitful bough, even a fruitful bough by a well; whose branches run over the wall:
>
> The archers have sorely grieved him, and shot at him, and hated him:
>
> But his bow abode in strength, and the arms of his hands were made strong by the hands of the mighty God of Jacob; (from thence is the shepherd, the stone of Israel:)
>
> Even by the God of thy father, who shall help thee; and by the Almighty, who shall bless thee with blessings of heaven above, blessings of the deep that lieth under, blessings of the breasts, and of the womb:
>
> The blessings of thy father have prevailed above the blessings of my progenitors unto the utmost bound of the everlasting hills: they shall be on the head of Joseph, and on the crown of the head of him that was separate from his brethren. (Genesis 49:22-26.)

The Book of Mormon makes it abundantly clear that America is the land of Joseph, who had two sons, both being heirs of his blessings. They were Ephraim and Manasseh. Their descendants would reach fruition in America, "in the utmost bounds of the everlasting hills."

Both Nephites and Lamanites are direct descendants

of Joseph through Lehi, who was of Manasseh, and Ishmael, who was of Ephraim. Ishmael and his family joined Lehi's family in the wilderness. When the daughters of Ishmael and the sons of Lehi married, the bloodlines were joined.

The brass plates of Laban revealed the lineage of Lehi, for it "came to pass that my father, Lehi, also found upon the plates of brass a genealogy of his fathers; wherefore he knew that he was a descendant of Joseph; yea, even that Joseph who was the son of Jacob, who was sold into Egypt, and who was preserved by the hand of the Lord, that he might preserve his father, Jacob, and all his household from perishing with famine.

"And they were also led out of captivity and out of the land of Egypt, by the same God who had preserved them.

"And thus my father, Lehi, did discover the genealogy of his fathers. And Laban also was a descendant of Joseph, wherefore he and his fathers had kept the records." (1 Nephi 5:14-16.)

When Jacob blessed Joseph that his descendants would "run over the wall," he meant that his family would go beyond Palestine, to America.

America is the Promised Land of the Western Hemisphere. Palestine is the Promised Land of the Eastern Hemisphere.

In the book of Jacob in the Book of Mormon, we have this interesting paragraph, which sustains our interpretation of the branches that "run over the wall":

"Wherefore, thus saith the Lord, I have led this people forth out of the land of Jerusalem, by the power of mine arm, that I might raise up unto me a righteous branch from the fruit of the loins of Joseph." (Jacob 2:25.)

When the Savior came among the Nephites he emphasized that the people living in America during that period were descendants of Joseph. But he said one additional thing: This land of America was given to the descendants of Joseph as an inheritance, given them directly by the Father. Said he:

"Ye are my disciples; and ye are a light unto this people, who are a remnant of the house of Joseph.

"And behold, this is the land of your inheritance; and the Father hath given it unto you." (3 Nephi 15:12-13.)

This was divine confirmation of the promise made by Lehi when he blessed his son Joseph in the wilderness, saying:

"And now I speak unto you, Joseph, my last-born. Thou wast born in the wilderness of mine afflictions; yea, in the days of my greatest sorrow did thy mother bear thee.

"And may the Lord consecrate also unto thee this land, which is a most precious land, for thine inheritance and the inheritance of thy seed with thy brethren, for thy security forever, if it so be that ye shall keep the commandments of the Holy One of Israel." (2 Nephi 3:1-2.)

And then we have this divine word regarding America and the descendants of Joseph: "Wherefore, I will consecrate this land unto thy seed, and them who shall be numbered among thy seed, forever, for the land of their inheritance; for it is a choice land, saith God unto me, above all other lands, wherefore I will have all men that dwell thereon that they shall worship me, saith God." (2 Nephi 10:19.)

The American inheritance of Joseph was so precious that the Lord spoke of this land as choice above all other lands, and promised that all who live here and serve him would not only prosper, but would be protected from all other nations. The scripture reads:

> And the Lord would not suffer that they should stop beyond the sea in the wilderness, but he would that they should come forth even unto the land of promise, which was choice above all other lands, which the Lord God had preserved for a righteous people.
>
> And he had sworn in his wrath unto the brother of Jared, that whoso should possess this land of promise, from that time henceforth and forever, should serve him, the true and only God, or they should be swept off when the fulness of his wrath should come upon them.
>
> And now, we can behold the decrees of God concerning this land, that it is a land of promise; and whatsoever nation shall possess it shall serve God, or they shall be swept off when the fulness of his

wrath shall come upon them. And the fulness of his wrath cometh upon them when they are ripened in iniquity.

For behold, this is a land which is choice above all other lands; wherefore he that doth possess it shall serve God or shall be swept off; for it is the everlasting decree of God. And it is not until the fulness of iniquity among the children of the land, that they are swept off. (Ether 2:7-10.)

He indicated that gentiles would be permitted to come here also, but gave them this warning:

And this cometh unto you, O ye Gentiles, that ye may know the decrees of God—that ye may repent, and not continue in your iniquities until the fulness come, that ye may not bring down the fulness of the wrath of God upon you as the inhabitants of the land have hitherto done.

Behold, this is a choice land, and whatsoever nation shall possess it shall be free from bondage, and from captivity, and from all other nations under heaven, if they will but serve the God of the land, who is Jesus Christ, who hath been manifested by the things which we have written. (Ether 2:11-12.)

The Savior predicted that on this land of Joseph—America—a mighty nation of the gentiles—the United States—would be set up as a land of freedom by the direct act of the Father (3 Nephi 21:4), and he revealed to the first Nephi the manner in which it would be done. (See 1 Nephi 13:1-19.)

The allotments to the Israelites in Palestine are very significant for many reasons. The people later were scattered and driven out of the land. But they will come back. The Jews are returning in accordance with the prophecies. The Lord said that before his second coming a *remnant* of the Jews would go back to Palestine, but not all of them. (See D&C 45.) Part of that remnant is there now—three million of them—and the gathering continues.

Joseph and Judah are accounted for, but the other ten tribes are "lost," and no revelation has indicated their whereabouts. The Prophet Joseph Smith did say that the apostle John was among them, preparing them for their return. (*History of the Church* 1:176.)

What about their return? This is explained in modern revelation. They will go back to their inheritances in

Palestine, but *before that* they will come to America and receive their blessings from Ephraim. Why? Because Ephraim is the tribe holding the birthright in Israel and hence has the right, through the priesthood, to administer the blessings of the gospel to all peoples. (See the entire section 133 of Doctrine and Covenants.)

Specifically the Lord says this about the lost tribes:

> And they who are in the north countries shall come in remembrance before the Lord; and their prophets shall hear his voice, and shall no longer stay themselves; and they shall smite the rocks, and the ice shall flow down at their presence.
>
> And an highway shall be cast up in the midst of the great deep.
>
> Their enemies shall become a prey unto them,
>
> And in the barren deserts there shall come forth pools of living water; and the parched ground shall no longer be a thirsty land.
>
> And they shall bring forth their rich treasures unto the children of Ephraim, my servants.
>
> And the boundaries of the everlasting hills shall tremble at their presence.
>
> And there shall they fall down and be crowned with glory, even in Zion, by the hands of the servants of the Lord, even the children of Ephraim.
>
> And they shall be filled with songs of everlasting joy.
>
> Behold, this is the blessing of the everlasting God upon the tribes of Israel, and the richer blessing upon the head of Ephraim and his fellows. (D&C 133:26-34.)

It will be in America—at Jackson County, Missouri—that the New Jerusalem will be built; and from there will the Lord govern the world during the Millennium. (See sections 45, 57, and 58 of the Doctrine and Covenants.)

Joseph was originally given an inheritance in Palestine. What will eventually become of that we do not know, but we are assured in revelation that the ultimate destiny and inheritance of both tribes of Joseph—Ephraim and Manasseh—will be in America.

Ephraim is widely scattered in the earth, but there is a heavy concentration of that blood in certain countries. For example, our stake patriarchs in Great Britain report that not more than 2 or 3 percent of the persons they bless are of any tribe *other* than Ephraim.

In Mexico, South America, and the Polynesian Islands,

the blood of Manasseh is rich, with millions of pure-blooded descendants of Lehi there, waiting for the gospel.

The blessings of Joseph truly flow "over the wall," and will see their great fulfillment in America.

Chapter 19

"CHOOSE YOU THIS DAY"

Joshua was now a hundred and ten years old. After reaching eighty, he undertook the greatest work of his life, with the help of the Lord, of course.

He had started with full assurance of divine help. The Lord promised that he would do for Joshua all that he had done for Moses; "only be strong and of a good courage," he was told.

And Joshua responded. The scripture says of him: "He left nothing undone of all that the Lord commanded Moses." (Joshua 11:15.)

But now he had accomplished his work. Israel was safely in the Promised Land. Most of the idolatrous and perverse nations had been destroyed. Only a few remained, and they were restrained by Israel. And "Joshua waxed old and stricken in age."

Knowing that death was near, he called to him "all Israel, and for their elders, and for their heads, and for their judges, and for their officers, and said unto them, I am old and stricken in age:

> And ye have seen all that the Lord your God hath done unto all these nations because of you; for the Lord your God is he that hath fought for you.
>
> Behold, I have divided unto you by lot these nations that remain, to be an inheritance for your tribes, from Jordan, with all the nations that I have cut off, even unto the great sea westward.
>
> And the Lord your God, he shall expel them from before you, and drive them from out of your sight; and ye shall possess their land, as the Lord your God hath promised unto you.
>
> Be ye therefore very courageous to keep and to do all that is written in the book of the law of Moses, that ye turn not aside therefrom to the right hand or to the left;
>
> That ye come not among these nations, these that remain among

you; neither make mention of the name of their gods, nor cause to swear by them, neither serve them, nor bow yourselves unto them:

But cleave unto the Lord your God, as ye have done unto this day. (Joshua 23:1-8.)

He again reminded them that it was by the power of God that they had been brought to Canaan and had cleansed it, adding: "Take good heed therefore unto yourselves, that ye love the Lord your God." (V. 11.) Then he gave them this warning:

Else if ye do in any wise go back, and cleave unto the remnant of these nations, even these that remain among you, and shall make marriages with them, and go in unto them, and they to you:

Know for a certainty that the Lord your God will no more drive out any of these nations from before you; but they shall be snares and traps unto you, and scourges in your sides, and thorns in your eyes, until ye perish from off this good land which the Lord your God hath given you.

And, behold, this day I am going the way of all the earth: and ye know in all your hearts and in all your souls, that not one thing hath failed of all the good things which the Lord your God spake concerning you; all are come to pass unto you, and not one thing hath failed thereof.

Therefore it shall come to pass, that as all good things are come upon you, which the Lord your God promised you; so shall the Lord bring upon you all evil things, until he have destroyed you from off this good land which the Lord your God hath given you.

When ye have transgressed the covenant of the Lord your God, which he commanded you, and have gone and served other gods, and bowed yourselves to them; then shall the anger of the Lord be kindled against you, and ye shall perish quickly from off the good land which he hath given unto you. (Vv. 12-16.)

Subsequently he called the people together again, repeating his warnings about following other gods and teaching again the great and safe principle that they must serve the true and living God.

Joshua said to them: "If ye forsake the Lord, and serve strange gods, then he will turn and do you hurt, and consume you, after that he hath done you good." (Joshua 24:20.)

Before he died, Joshua wanted to place his people under covenant to serve the Lord and forsake all other gods. Hence he said:

"Now therefore fear the Lord, and serve him in sincerity and in truth: and put away the gods which your fathers served on the other side of the flood, and in Egypt; and serve ye the Lord.

"And if it seem evil unto you to serve the Lord, choose you this day whom ye will serve; whether the gods which your fathers served that were on the other side of the flood, or the gods of the Amorites, in whose land ye dwell: but as for me and my house, we will serve the Lord." (Vv. 14-15.)

The people cried out to Joshua: "God forbid that we should forsake the Lord, to serve other gods. . . . Nay; but we will serve the Lord." (Vv. 16, 21.)

So Joshua made a covenant with them that day and said to the people: "Ye are witnesses against yourselves that ye have chosen you the Lord, to serve him." (V. 22.)

And the people replied: "We are witnesses."

Then says the scripture:

> And Joshua wrote these words in the book of the law of God, and took a great stone, and set it up there under an oak, that was by the sanctuary of the Lord.
>
> And Joshua said unto all the people, Behold, this stone shall be a witness unto us; for it hath heard all the words of the Lord which he spake unto us: it shall be therefore a witness unto you, lest ye deny your God.
>
> So Joshua let the people depart, every man unto his inheritance.
>
> And it came to pass after these things, that Joshua the son of Nun, the servant of the Lord, died, being an hundred and ten years old.
>
> And they buried him in the border of his inheritance in Timnathserah, which is in mount Ephraim, on the north side of the hill of Gaash.
>
> And Israel served the Lord all the days of Joshua, and all the days of the elders that overlived Joshua, and which had known all the works of the Lord, that he had done for Israel. (Joshua 24:26-31.)

In the midst of the most severe opposition, spiritually and physically, Joshua had led Israel. Here was a man who did not question the Lord, who did everything he was commanded to do, and who set an example for Israel that they much too quickly forgot.

He was an exemplar of the true meaning of the first

and great commandments of the Lord. He was a pattern to live by. "As for me and my house, we will serve the Lord."

Chapter 20

THE BIBLE IS HISTORY

Archaeology is proving the Bible to be correct in its history, and modern revelation sustains it fully "as far as it is translated correctly." We, therefore, may fully accept the story of Joshua as it is presented therein.

The Dead Sea Scrolls, of course, constitute the most exciting of the more recent finds confirming the writings of the scripture, but many other discoveries are now placing the facts of biblical history beyond the reach of the critics. The Bible is true.

As *The Romance of Archaeology* puts it: "Archaeology has converted both laity and clergy. No longer do they fear that archaeological investigation will overturn Biblical statements. Thus far the finds have confirmed them, or have opened confirmatory possibilities." (R. V. D. Magoffin and Emily C. Davis, Garden City, New York: Garden City Publishing Company, 1929, p. 82.)

The spade has thrown new light on scripture and on biblical personalities from Abraham to Peter and Paul. These finds have added great support to the scriptural writings.

Note just a few of the discoveries:

Though for a long time scholars thought the city of Ur existed only in fable, now through an accident its ruins have been found and excavated. It is discovered to have been a city with many modern conveniences, such as spacious homes, running water inside some houses, bathrooms with tubs and flush toilets, and libraries containing thousands of cuneiform tablets.

The city of Mari, also in Abrahamic country, has been unearthed, with its temples and palaces and hundreds of masonry homes. The area had an irrigation system and raised bounteous crops. Thousands of clay tablets found there tell the story. Some cuneiform tablets contain as many as 2,000 names of craftsmen and their guilds or unions. This city was destroyed by invasion in 1700 B.C.

The palace alone covered 10 acres and had 800 rooms which were divided into 260 apartments, many with open courtyards. Although 13,000 clay tablets were found in the palace, more than 23,000 tablets were found in the main library.

An old Babylonian inscription was found there indicating not only that there was a flood in Noah's time, but also that Mari was the tenth city to be built after the flood.

Haran, the home of Abraham, is mentioned in tablets found there. Nahor has been found also.

As Werner Keller in his *The Bible as History* expresses it, "The documents from the kingdom of Mari produce startling proof again that the stories of the patriarchs in the Bible are not pious legends, as is often too readily assumed, but events that are described as happening in a historical period that can be precisely dated." (New York: Wm. Morrow & Co., 1956, p. 52.)

Another Abrahamic city, Shechem, has been found in excavations at Tell Balata.

Ancient Nineveh has been discovered and found to be a great center of education and business. The library of King Ashurbanipal alone contained 22,000 texts.

Evidences of the flood of Noah's day have been found in several locations by digging in deposits of clay. Relics of a civilization dating before the flood are found beneath the clay and evidences of later civilizations are found above it.

Various accounts of the flood are given in Indian, Chaldean, Persian, and Greek literature.

As far back as 1866, when the Palestine Exploration fund was set up, interest in Palestinian research developed; and when the Moabite Stone was discovered in 1868 and George Smith published fragments of the

Babylonian flood story, "Palestine became a sensation," say Magoffin and Davis.

The Moabite Stone was found in 1868 at Dibon. It had been erected in 850 B.C. to commemorate a victory in the revolt of King Mesha of Moab against Israel. Fragments of this stone are now in the Louvre.

To quote the *Romance of Archaeology* further:

"When the late George Smith made sensational finds at Kouyunjik in the Euphrates valley of certain tablets now known as the 'Creation Tablets' and the 'Deluge Tablets,' the Near East past rose from the dead. The synthetic thunder produced by archaeology and the revivifying lightning forged by scholarly Vulcans, after blowing the ashes of the forgotten past off the glowing facts below, heralded the Aurora which today would be screened in the vivid words: 'Came the Dawn' of Biblical archaeology." (P. 75.)

As mentioned earlier, the ancient city of Jericho, not far from its modern location, has been found and excavated. Dr. Kathleen M. Kenyon, director of the British School of Archaeology in Jerusalem, believes that the city originally dates back probably 7,000 years, definitely 5,000, and she says that it can lay claim justly to the honor of being "by far the oldest city in the world."

Another of the truly ancient cities of Palestine, mentioned several times in the Bible and conquered repeatedly over the centuries, is Lachish. That city was one of the larger and more important ones in Palestine over the centuries. Instead of the six to ten acres occupied by most of those cities, Lachish occupied twenty-four acres. An inscription on a bowl found by research crews indicates the city was conquered by Israel in 1230 B.C.

Harper's Bible Dictionary says of Lachish:

> Lachish was the enormously important stronghold which every aggressor from the S. had to control before advancing on Jerusalem. Lachish (once erroneously located by Flinders Petrie at Tell el-Hesi, where he worked out his amazing "yardstick" of pottery), the fortress city on the Tell ed-Duweir site, was the scene of one of the three greatest archaeological investigations in Palestine.

It was explored by the Wellcome-Marston Archaeological Research Expedition, headed first (1932-1938) by J. L. Starkey, one of the ablest technicians in the field, whose work was tragically interrupted when he was murdered by a brigand just when the careful preparatory work involved in a total clearance process was beginning to yield amazing treasures of historical information.

Work was continued by O. Tufnell, C. H. Inge, Lankester Harding, and others. Evidence dug from the massive mound of buried history sheds light on successive epochs from Late Bronze Age cave-dwellers, whose pottery studio and tools were found in a cave, on through the Biblical periods, especially the years just prior to the Exile.

Evidences of the occupation of Lachish by Hyksos horsemen (1720-1550 B.C., in Egypt) have been found, in a typical deep fosse or defense ditch with almost perpendicular sides, that provided an enclosure (possibly for horses) with a ramp of clay and lime. In that fosse were found three later Canaanite-Egyptian temples, built between c. 1475 and 1223 B.C. (P. 375.)

Sir Charles Marston, British archaeologist, indicates in his book *The Bible Comes Alive* that he considers the Lachish excavations among the most important in all Palestine. For example, an old Babylonian cylinder-seal (for sealing official documents) from the middle of the third millennium B.C. has an illustration that resembles a picture of the fall of Adam. It shows a god, a tree of life, a woman, and a snake.

An alabaster vase, found at the site of biblical Erech and also dating to the third millennium B.C., shows in relief the offering of sacrifices of fruit and lambs.

On a wall in a tomb in Memphis, Egypt, is a bas-relief showing a group of foreigners bowing before a high ranking Egyptian, recalling the story of Joseph and his brothers in Egypt. The foreigners' facial features are obviously Semite.

In a wall painting inside a tomb at Thebes, Semites are seen at work making bricks and building a granary.

One of the actual bricks from that day has been found, made of clay from the Nile and containing straw. A stamp on the surface of the brick bears the sovereign seal of Ramses II who probably lived during the Israelitish period of slavery.

A bas-relief found in a tomb at Saqqara shows young men being circumcised with a stone knife.

In many parts of Palestine archaeologists have found images of Ashtaroth, the naked fertility goddess of the Canaanites; images of the god Baal have also been found in various locations.

In Transjordan a basalt stela has been found telling of the military campaign of King Mesha of Moab against Israel, again confirming the Bible. The Moabite stone refers to this same King Mesha.

A basalt obelisk over six feet high has been found in Assyria; it tells of Shalmaneser II defeating Israel and says that King Jehu of Israel paid tribute to this Assyrian king, again confirming the Bible.

Found at Megiddo was a seal belonging to the time of Jeroboam II, who reigned from 787 to 747 B.C. The seal shows a roaring lion, and above the animal it reads: "Servant of Jeroboam."

A stone tablet marks the grave of King Uzziah.

An inscription on stone has been found telling of the victory of King Sargon II of Assyria in his campaign against Palestine. Part of the inscription reads: "I besieged and captured Samaria and carried off 27,290 of its inhabitants as booty."

A bas-relief found in Nineveh shows the campaign against Samaria in 721 B.C.

An inscription written in ancient Hebrew characters was found in the famous tunnel built by King Hezekiah, briefly telling of the difficulty of boring the tunnel to preserve the city's water supply.

In a bas-relief King Sennacherib is shown seated on his throne in front of the city of Lachish in Judea, again confirming that siege.

A hexagonal prism has been found engraved in cuneiform, telling of Sennacherib's campaign of 701 B.C. against Judah.

Another inscription has been found telling of Nebuchadnezzar's invasion of the Holy Land in 599 B.C., confirming the story of Zedekiah, so well known in the Bible. This was in the time of Lehi.

Two fragments of clay tablets have been found in Babylon listing the rations given to the Jewish prisoners during the Babylonian captivity.

Hebrew coins have been found dating back to the old kingdom of Judah.

The copper mines and smelters of Solomon have been found and used in a modern experiment. Evidence of his stables has been uncovered also.

The story of the Queen of Sheba visiting Solomon has been verified, although for many years it was considered a myth.

Archaeologists now affirm that they have evidence that man's first religion was monotheism, and that the introduction of many gods came later as a part of a retrogression of some branches of the human race.

Sir Flinders Petrie's excavations in old Gaza indicate that gold ornaments found there came from Ireland, and he suggests that trade with Ireland began before the days of Abraham. Gaza was the seaport that connected the mainland with Crete.

As the years go by, and as more digging is done, the doubts about the historicity of the Bible are fast disappearing. The scripture now successfully resists all attacks made upon its integrity.

Chapter 21

COMPANION SCRIPTURES

When the Prophet Joseph Smith prepared to send missionaries westward from Kirtland, twelve of the elders met together for their instructions before departing.

On February 9, 1831, the Lord gave a revelation to the Prophet for the guidance of these missionaries; among other things he said: "And again, the elders, priests and teachers of this church shall teach the principles of my gospel, which are in the Bible and the Book of Mormon, in the which is the fulness of the gospel." (D&C 42:12.)

Nothing was said at this time about accepting the Bible "as far as it is translated correctly." That came later, and with good reason.

But here is a direct statement from the Lord to the effect that between the Bible and the Book of Mormon the fulness of the gospel may be found and from them it should be preached! Does not that make the Bible fully acceptable to us, his people?

He mentioned the Bible first. We name it first in our Articles of Faith wherein we say: "We believe the Bible to be the word of God as far as it is translated correctly; we also believe the Book of Mormon to be the word of God." (Article of Faith 8.)

The Lord gave us these two "sticks": the stick of Judah and the stick of Joseph. (Ezekiel 37:15-20.) They sustain each other. The prophet said that we of latter days would hold the two as one in our hands.

When the Prophet Joseph declared that there were errors in the translation of the Bible, of course he was correct. He studied Hebrew in order to better understand the Old Testament in its original language.

The mistakes in the earliest translations of the Bible were legion, some of them deliberate, others from poor work on the part of the printers.

It seems unthinkable that any man or set of men would deliberately change the text of the word of God to further their own selfish ends. Yet it was done, and repeatedly, as the early versions of the Bible were distributed.

The Church of England published its Bishop's Bible as a means of combating some of the biased versions brought out by the protestors of that day.

The Wycliffe Bible, whose translator brought it out under the worst kind of persecution in 1380, was an honest effort to present the word of God in such a way that it could be understood by the common people. But even that Bible reflected the translator's personal views. This was true of the Tyndale Bible of 1525 and the Matthews Bible of 1537 and the Taveners Bible of 1539.

When the Douay version, or the Vulgate, appeared in 1582, it presented the point of view of the Roman Catholic Church. When Dr. J. P. Arendzen, under assignment of the Roman Catholic hierarchy of Great Britain, produced his 1947 revision of the Douay Bible, he frankly said in the preface that it was done because the 1582 version carried too much of the Reformation flavor.

In 1965, while the Catholic Church in England was waiting for the completion of its own modern translation, permission was sought and obtained to produce a Catholic edition of the Revised Standard Version of the Protestants; this was published in England in 1965. It contains many changes. The preface says:

"For four hundred years, following the great upheaval of the Reformation, Catholics and Protestants have gone their separate ways and suspected each other's translations of the Bible of having been in some way manipulated in the interests of doctrinal pre-suppositions. It must be admitted that these suspicions were not always without foundation."

Some writers allege that in Oliver Cromwell's day he bribed the printers with a thousand pounds sterling to falsify the text in one edition to support the Cromwell party in its efforts to have the clergy elected by the congregations.

In one of the poorly printed early English Bibles, the seventh commandment reads: "Thou shalt commit adultery"; and Paul's announcement to the Corinthians (1 Corinthians 6:9) appeared as "The unrighteous shall inherit the Kingdom of Heaven."

Not until the Oxford standard edition of the King James Bible appeared did we have a text of the Authorized Version such as we have today. But even then errors persisted. Where in Numbers we are told "the murderer shall surely be put to death," it read "the murderer shall surely be put together."

And speaking of murderers, the 1801 printing of Jude 16 read "murderers" instead of the correct "murmurers."

We in The Church of Jesus Christ of Latter-day Saints today accept the present King James Bible as the official Bible of our church, and with good reason. That reason is the Book of Mormon itself, which quotes many Bible passages almost precisely as they appear in the King James Bible. Some have thought that Joseph Smith copied those sections out of the Bible and inserted them in the Book of Mormon, which is not true.

No one reading the beautiful language of the Savior, for example, or the heroic defense of Abinadi, both of whom entwine their own words with quotations from the prophets, would ever suppose that Joseph Smith was capable of doing such a thing.

At the time the Book of Mormon was translated, Joseph was a very unlearned man, just as Isaiah said he would be (Isaiah 29), and was in no way qualified either as a writer or as an editor. He translated the gold plates as he was given power by God, pure and simple. Those Bible quotations were originally from the brass plates; then in Mormon's day they were placed on the gold plates; and from the gold plates Joseph Smith translated them for publication in the Book of Mormon.

The Book of Mormon is the strongest testimonial there is to the general accuracy of the King James Version. Read, for example, the twenty-fourth chapter of Third Nephi, and examine the quotations from Malachi. Or read the Sermon on the Mount, and compare it with the King James rendering.

The Isaiah chapters were direct translations of that early prophet's writings, as they were transmitted first by means of the brass plates and then the gold.

There are minor problems with the new translations of some passages in the Bible, and none of them agree word for word. But the real meaning is there for the most part. When the various new translations are compared, no one need mistake the intent of the original writer. To obtain the proper understanding is the main thing. And where there is still any question, we always have reference to our modern scriptures and our living prophets.

Unless he expected the Bible to be used, believed, and preached, the Lord would never have spoken as he did to the twelve elders leaving for their mission westward from Kirtland. (D&C 42:12.)

And this, of course, means that we accept the Bible account of Moses and Joshua, the miracles in which they were involved, and the covenants they made with the people of the Lord.

What wonderful direction we find in Joshua's words: "As for me and my house, we will serve the Lord."

As we read the story of his great career, we may know that it really happened—because the modern scriptures tell us so, and they are true!

INDEX